W9-DJE-727

Jɑ

WITHDRAWN

SEX ATTITUDES IN THE HOME

RALPH G. ECKERT

Sex Attitudes
in the Home

ASSOCIATION PRESS

NEW YORK

Carl A. Rudisill Library
LENOIR RHYNE COLLEGE

Ec5a
35,187
July 1957

SEX ATTITUDES IN THE HOME

Copyright © 1956 by
National Board of Young Men's Christian Associations

Association Press, 291 Broadway, New York 7, N. Y.

612.6
Ec5S

Library of Congress catalog card number: 56-6450

55

Printed in the United States of America
American Book–Stratford Press, Inc., New York

35187

*To my wife, Elizabeth Flinn Eckert,
who is really co-author of this book,
and to our three teen-agers who gave
us the courage to write it.*

What This Book Is About . . .

$\mathcal{T}$his is a book about sex attitudes in the home and the opportunities parents have to create in their growing children positive feelings about sex. Feelings about sex—not merely the facts of sex—are powerful determinants of behavior, and good attitudes toward sex strengthen good relations in home and community.

What This Book Attempts to Do

The purpose of this book is to help parents approach the sex education of their children constructively and with confidence. Some of the stages through which children go in the process of maturing are indicated; and learning experiences, naturally related to each of these stages, are suggested.

Numerous illustrations are given in which parents

have used situations to improve sex knowledge and feelings, in the hope that this will help the reader to be creative in the situations he faces. The realization that it is possible to learn from mistakes as well as from success helps one to try to do his best. Children have the bounce of a rubber ball and can be most forgiving. They give their parents chance after chance, and most parents make good in the end. Doing "something" with confidence is far better than the old pattern of fearfully doing nothing, or doing "too little and too late."

An annotated bibliography is supplied on page 239, because reading and word-of-mouth education on sex, as on any other subject, are supplementary to each other. Reference is made also in the text to useful books and films. The reader will find documentation for these on page 243, where they are listed alphabetically by title.

What This Book Is Not

Sex Attitudes in the Home is not a blueprint to be followed exactly. The incidents here described are not meant to indicate *the way* to handle such situations, but merely one way. No two persons can or should react in exactly the same manner. No two persons have the same experiences or vocabulary upon which to draw. Other people's ideas and experiences can often be helpful, but it is important for parents to be free to handle situations in the way that they *feel* is right.

This book is not a schedule for parents to follow. Children have their own built-in timetables. They mature at different rates and they have different experiences along the way. The ages mentioned in these chapters more nearly represent stages. Children vary markedly in their interests, and the same child differs greatly from time to time.

No attempt is made here to cover every facet of sex relatedness, for sex permeates almost every phase of life. In addition, it is a fact that the sexual aspects of personality vary from individual to individual as much as intelligence, height, weight, responsiveness, or emotional stability. Generalizations are based upon large groups, but individual variations in every direction are expected as normal.

Much That Can Be Done by Parents

We can all be happier and more creative persons as we free ourselves from the unwholesome fears of earlier generations. With better understanding and with more positive attitudes ourselves, we shall sense many opportunities to share insights and feelings with our growing children.

But good intentions are not enough! Attitudes

toward sex are too important to leave to chance or to other people's children. Our children need *our* guidance. There is much that can be done. It is hoped that this book will help.

Contents

CHAPTER 1

A Positive Approach to Sex

Parents can approach the sex education of their children more positively if they first ask themselves some questions: What do we really want our children to know and to feel about sex? How can we help them experience the joy and the cost of being alive, of belonging, of being cared about, of caring about others? Will they know deep inside that the way they act makes a difference to the ongoing process of creation? Will they feel free to come to us with their problems? Shall we be able to give them the sort of feeling that Mark, a twelve-year-old boy, experienced when, after hearing the talk of some older boys, he went one day to his father with his confusions?

"As my father talked with me that day," Mark later recalled, "I suddenly sensed that I was the living expression of the love of my father and mother for each other. Even my body seemed to take on a new significance. I had respected and cared for it as a boy does who aspires to become an athlete. But that I had within me the power to create a new human being seemed almost too wonderful."

Good Feelings About Sex

Being born a boy or a girl means that one's parents and society expect a certain pattern of behavior, a pattern which varies from culture to culture, from group to group, and from family to family. In our American culture parents share responsibility for helping their children to become self-accepting boys and girls, socially competent adolescents, mutually understanding husbands and wives, and loving fathers and mothers.

Lacking a real understanding of sex, young people tend to accept without question, or to rebel blindly against, existing patterns of sexual behavior. If parents wish to help their children make wise choices—upon the basis of reasoned self-control and long-range values—they must become more understanding of sexual development in all its aspects, and more appreciative of the positive values of love-sex feelings. If parents can share their own good feelings for the sexual side of life and love and their own increasing understanding of it, they will improve not only their

[2]

children's chances for a satisfying life but those of their children's children.

What Children Need

Children need to know the sexual facts of life and love. But they need also to develop their capacity to care about others. And although they care, they still cannot be counted upon to act wisely unless they develop a sense of right and wrong—a conscience. And even if they know the facts, care about others, and have a sense of right and wrong, they still need the ability to understand their impulses and control their behavior in terms of moral values. These qualities we call character. All these aspects of personality must be developed during the long trek of youth to maturity.

Fortunately, parents have many opportunities and many years in which to help their children achieve these important goals. It is never too early to begin. They may wish they could start again, but all people have to begin where they are, and go on from there. There is no choice as to whether or not a parent will influence his children's development—he is bound to do so—but he has considerable choice as to *how* he will influence it. A parent may pass on his own feelings and attitudes without realizing that he is doing so; or he may choose to become increasingly aware of what is happening in his sexual development. He

[3]

can be honest with his real feelings and their relation to his own behavior. He can try to understand what experiences have caused him to think and feel as he does. A parent can become clearer as to what he really values.

Sex Education—a Lifelong Process

Most parents realize that their children are going to get a sex education. The only question is, "What kind of sex education will they get—and from whom?" The answer is not simple, for they will acquire it from every experience that makes them feel loved or rejected, appreciated or scorned, competent or inadequate as a male or a female. The world is their classroom—their own feelings and the human beings they meet, their teachers. And yet, because parents are with them most; because they have the most natural occasions to make their children feel comfortable about being boys and girls; because they have a continuing opportunity to create an environment in which natural curiosity is encouraged, not feared, in which sex feelings are accepted and increasingly understood, and in which the satisfactions of marriage and family life are experienced and observed—because of all these privileges, parents are by far the most important teachers their children will ever have.

What children learn from their parents depends in

large measure upon how they feel about their fathers and mothers—or perhaps more accurately—*how children think their parents feel about them.* For example, Alan, a fourteen-year-old boy, was in bed with pneumonia. His mother was amazed to see him looking so happy. A little questioning revealed the surprising fact that Alan had realized for the first time by his father's concern and behavior, that his father really loved him. His father was horrified to hear this. For years he had wanted only the best for his only son. Apparently, however, in constantly trying to help his son improve, he had given Alan the feeling of always falling short of his father's aspirations—the feeling that he was loved not *for what he was,* but only for what his father hoped he might become. The boy had almost stopped trying.

It has been said that the greatest thing parents can do for their children is to enjoy them. To grow up capable of loving others, a child needs to feel that someone loves him *as he is.* Ideally, of course, parents do this. If their relationship with the child is mutually satisfying and enriching, life is like that for both. If it is not, the child will try many ways to win love from someone. He may even resort to illness or destructiveness or some other effort that bids for attention.

The child has a good many formative years in which the parents can build in him self-acceptance,

[5]

self-confidence, and self-control before the physiological development of adolescence and the dating and courtship period make sex a central factor in personality development and social relationships. As the child feels that his family care about him, he learns to respond by caring about them, and then about others outside the family. Sex relations become just one aspect of the much bigger field of human relations. Impulses become increasingly subordinated to long-range goals; personal desires, to shared planning.

Sex—a Powerful Force in Life

Not understanding sex adequately, human beings have often feared this powerful force. Sex can embarrass, it can be used to exploit and to hurt. When misused, it can destroy the good feeling that once existed between two persons; it can change happiness into unhappiness; it can turn love into hate. And it is clear, too, what abuse of sex can do to the self-esteem of both the exploiter and the exploited.

All these statements are true, but they are only a small part of the big story. To at least some extent most human beings use sex constructively throughout their lives. They grow up to be relatively warm, affectionate, and responsible human beings. With more help from wholesome adults youth could grow up more wholesomely. And most people could be happier if they more truly appreciated the power for good that sex can become.

There is probably no greater force for socializing and humanizing the individual than the positive feelings which orient him toward a particular member of the other sex. Gradually, the child grows from the dependence of childhood into the independence of adolescence. Just when it seems that he is to become an impossible individualist, he usually decides that independence is not so satisfying as *inter*dependence. Impelled by the desire to relate intimately with a member of the other sex, he learns to control and re-direct his impulses in ways which improve his relations with the other sex. This experience normally helps him to improve his relations with his own sex, with adults in general, and even with his own parents. We know, too, that sex has the power to attract —and to help hold together—a man and woman, so that our family structure has its basis in these positive love-sex feelings.

Love-sex feelings are also a powerful stimulus to achievement. Spurred by the desire for intimacy and a home and family of his own, the young man directs his energy into vocational effort and achievement. Recently an easygoing adolescent, he now throws himself into the task of getting an education, learning salable skills, and acquiring more mature work habits.

We know, too, the power of love-sex intimacy to enrich the relationship between two individuals as they face together the innumerable and inevitable frustrations and irritations of everyday life. Good feelings generated between them dim the petty annoyances of family living. An attitude of forgiveness changes not the facts but the feelings about them and allows the couple to forget the past and look confidently toward the future in a spirit of togetherness.

Sex contains the power to create life in all its forms. The world's greatest scientists cannot produce a single living cell—but a man and a woman together have the divine privilege of creating a human being. Few other events can contain so much satisfaction as the arrival, and life, of an individual who comes into the world as the fulfillment of a deep love two persons feel for each other.

CHAPTER 2

Curiosity—Doorway to Understanding

Carefully the mother had placed an old blanket on the back lawn. Then, even more carefully, she had placed her diapered seven-month-old boy in the center. They smiled at each other. Mother was pleased with her idea. Donny could get sun and fresh air, and she could dig a bit among the plants that surrounded the lawn—and so she dug.

But Donny, being a baby, did not stay quiet long. A series of wiggling movements brought him to the edge of the blanket. There he stopped and surveyed the green grass in front of him. Cautiously he reached out and touched it. After another moment his tiny hand closed on some grass and he transported it to his mouth.

Unfortunately, at that moment, Donny's mother glanced in his direction. "No, Donny," she cried, "you mustn't put the dirty grass in your mouth." Hurriedly she wiped the grass off his hand and put him back in the center of the blanket. Within the next fifteen minutes, the "act" was repeated several times before she finally gave up and took him back into the house.

It was as natural for Donny to head for the grass as to breathe. He was exploring this great wonderful universe in which he found himself. Had his curiosity been allowed to run its course, he would have touched the grass. Finding it pleasant to the touch, he would then have tried it out for taste. Not finding it particularly pleasant to either taste or touch in the mouth he would have looked for other worlds to conquer. But because his exploration was interrupted, he returned to his investigation again and again until there was one frustrated mother and one frustrated child.

Why are some parents so delighted when the baby plays with his toes, yet so uncomfortable when he discovers his penis? It, too, is part of this wonderful body of his, and he must explore its sensations. Cries of "dirty" will probably no more stop him from exploring his penis than Donny from exploring the grass. But if his exploring makes a parent uncomfortable enough, the child may become uncomfortable too. He may learn to explore when no one is around, but feel uncomfortable and guilty about it.

One young father was surprised to note that his four-year-old son, sitting on the toilet while daddy shaved, was unself-consciously handling his erect little penis. The father's first reaction was to stop him; his second, to continue his shaving; and so he did. As a matter of fact, he felt pleased that his son was free to handle his genitals in his presence. At least he had not made him feel guilty about it; and he was determined he would not. He finished shaving, his son finished his toileting, mother called them to breakfast, and the incident was past. A child had explored the sensations of his own body. No barrier had been raised to mar the comfortable relationship of this boy and his father. Another father might have diverted his son by suggesting that he wash his hands and be ready for breakfast when mother called. Still another might have dealt with the problem by asking the child if his clothes were too tight. There is no one way to handle such situations. Honesty of feeling, coupled with consideration for the child's feeling, would seem to be the best policy.

But will a child not develop the "habit" of manipulating his genitals if his parents do not stop him? What does one mean by a habit? His penis will probably always yield a certain amount of pleasure, so he may be expected to repeat from time to time. But so does eating yield pleasure, so does playing, so later will reading, television, and a host of other interests.

If the child is discovered returning again and again to his penis for satisfaction, it may be on a par with the frequent sucking of his thumb for comfort. The question for the parent to ask himself in either case should probably be, "Why is he not receiving a wider range of satisfactions in other activities?" Since nothing happens without an adequate cause, "What need is he satisfying by this behavior?" "Is this a substitute for affection, attention, activity, security, adventure, or a sense of achievement?" The parent then can direct his or her efforts constructively to guide the child toward more acceptable ways of satisfying these needs.

Building Favorable Attitudes
Toward Sex Differences

Sooner or later each child is going to discover that some children have different sex organs from his own. He is going to be curious to see what they look like. The child who has been fortunate enough to have brothers and sisters with whom to bathe during the preschool years observes and takes these differences in stride.

Most nursery schools and kindergartens, as a matter of policy, use a single toileting facility. Experience has proved that curiosity can thus be satisfied naturally. One nursery-school teacher reported a new four-year-old girl, who had no brothers, noticing first that boys stood up at the toilet like her daddy. The second day she walked up to a boy who was urinating and, leaning forward, looked at his penis. She straightened up, smiled at him, and said pleasantly, "Well, you are a boy, aren't you!" Then she went on about her own toileting—satisfied.

When little girls first observe that little boys can go to the toilet standing up, they sometimes try to do the same, with uncomfortable results. One mother reported her only child's coming home from kindergarten, where the children shared a common toilet, and commenting that the boys didn't have to sit down to urinate—why did she? Mother and daughter spent a profitable half hour talking about sex differences.

Parents are often surprised to discover that a child has somehow gotten the idea that he, or she, will change sex in the process of growing up. One father was surprised by a question fired at him as he entered the bathroom. His four-year-old daughter and five-year-old son were bathing together and obviously had been having an argument. "Daddy, I will too have a penis when I grow up, won't I?" his daughter asked. The father was somewhat taken aback, but rallied his forces and replied as calmly and as casually as he could. "Why, no, darling. Only little boys have penises." She looked thoughtful a moment and then said, "And girls have vaginas, don't they?"

She said it with about as much enthusiasm as she would have said, "Boys have motorcycles and girls have tricycles, don't they?" The father sensed this feeling of having a poor substitute and felt that something had to be done—but what? Then he had an inspiration.

"Yes, darling, you have a vagina. But you know you have some other very wonderful things that Billy doesn't have. Only they are inside where you can't see them." He closed the lid of the toilet and sat down. He told her about the uterus (or womb as it is called in the Bible). He told her this was a very special place for babies to grow in until they are big enough to eat and drink for themselves, when they are born. He told it very simply, at the four-year level of understanding. At the conclusion she looked at him and asked, "Does Billy have a . . . what do you call it?" "A uterus—no, Billy doesn't have a uterus. Only girls have uteruses. And only women can have babies." "Good," she concluded the lesson, with a satisfied smile.

A few days later, the little girl's mother was surprised by a comment the child made while helping her in the kitchen, as only a four-year-old can help. "You know, Mommy, I'm glad I'm a little girl. 'Cause when I grow up into a woman, I'll be able to have a baby—but Billy won't." Father had done a good job. At four, his little girl, instead of feeling cheated because she hadn't been given a penis, was glad that she was a girl, and had a good feeling about someday being a mother.

The important thing seems to be to help little girls realize that they have something wonderful too—only it is inside. One mother felt perhaps she had gone too far in making her daughter feel good about being a girl, when her boy complained bitterly that he didn't feel it was fair that only women could have babies. But she used the opportunity to help him accept the fact that men and women are different in many ways, and that there are advantages enjoyed by both sexes.

In another case, a little boy was watching his Aunt Mary change his baby cousin. Noting that the baby had no penis, he asked anxiously, "Did she lose her wee-wee?" Aunt Mary was able to assure him that she had not lost it—had never had one, in fact. Little girls don't. "Good," he concluded. "I wouldn't want to lose mine." He might have worried about that had she not helped him accept sex differences.

Her handling of his question, truthfully and simply, was quite in contrast to that of the woman who was asked by her little daughter what that "thing" was on her new baby brother. "Oh, it's just something the doctor forgot to cut off at the hospital," said she, trying to pass it off casually. Her daughter disappeared and returned with the big butcher knife. "Let's cut it off," she insisted. Mother had not only missed an excellent opportunity to begin building an acceptance of sex difference, but had created a serious misconception.

Sex Play—Unsatisfied Needs?

Children are interested in anything new or different. One should not be surprised, therefore, at attempts to observe or inquire about their own sex organs and those of others. If parents realize that some sex play is almost universal among children, they will not be so shocked or so quick to blame participants.

There are better ways than sex play to satisfy curiosity. And when sex play results from other unsatisfied needs, such as the need for attention or perhaps just the need for something to do, there are other constructive alternatives. Sensitivity to children's personality needs, plenty of opportunities for interesting activity, plus a reasonable amount of adult supervision are among the best preventives of sex play.

When sex play does occur, what then? Attempts to frighten children nearly always have harmful after-effects—usually at the unconscious or unobservable level. Take the extreme case of the mother who discovered her little boy and two little neighbor girls, all about five, undressed, up in his playroom. She was greatly shocked, and put on a terrific act for the children. She sent the two little girls home, telling them never to come back. She then got out her suit-case and began packing it, telling her son she was going away, that she just could not live with such a "bad" little boy. She put on her hat and coat and started for the door. He clung to her and pleaded with her hysterically not to leave him. She finally agreed on the condition that he would never do any-thing "terrible" like that again. She could not under-stand later why this boy became shy and uncomfort-able around girls.

Quite in contrast was the mother who discovered a group of children of the four-to-six range all un-dressed in the garage. She saw their embarrassment at being "caught" and relieved their feelings by say-ing, "It's all right to be curious about each other's bodies. Most children are. If you'll all get dressed and come into the house, I'll read you *The Wonderful Story of How You Were Born.*"

What to do and *how* to do it depends on the par-ents, on the children, on the mother's relationship with other mothers in the neighborhood, and so on. It might be better, in some instances, for each mother to talk with her own child alone later.

One mother of six children said that when she was at her wit's end, if she could only remember how much she loved them, and if she could remember that faith could move mountains, the scene would suddenly shift. She could then react constructively.

Parents sometimes need to learn to trust their feelings—not necessarily their first surface reaction, which may well be one of consternation, but their deeper feelings of caring and of confidence in their children.

Answering Children's Questions

Not all questions are asked in words. Not all answers are given in words. How can parents improve communication so that they get through to their children? It is not just factual information about the origins of life that a child needs. What he wants to know most of all is that he is loved and wanted, just as he is, his growing self. Children have a great sense of "growth." It saves them from their present helplessness and inadequacy. Helping a child to develop this sense of growth by showing him pictures of his former "littler self" and helping to minimize his sense of failure when he tackles something too difficult is constructive. One young father told that his five-year-old Danny, when he found himself unable to do what he had seen his seven-year-old brother do, said, "I just can't do it, Daddy—but I'll be able to do it next year, won't I?" His father assured him that he would—and Danny did.

Life offers limitless opportunities to develop this sense of growth in a child and relate it to his own beginnings. Seeing some tiny baby guppies, it is easy to say reverently, "Do you know, you were that tiny once upon a time, when you were still growing inside your mother, long before you were born?" Farm children have the opportunity to see and sense growth all about them, but children may miss much unless they are encouraged. City parents may need to plan how they can best develop their children's awareness of living things. Driving a few miles out of the way to visit a chicken farm so that the children can watch baby chicks breaking out of eggs, and look at hundreds of chickens, from the tiniest, still fastened to the yolk sac, to larger and larger sizes as they grow up, may start them thinking. Taking a child to the zoo in the spring when the various babies are being born, going back again and again to the child's favorite, taking and comparing snapshots during the summer months, finding out from *Being Born* or other books in the library how long the various animal babies have to grow inside the mother before they are ready to be born (ranging from a few weeks to two years) helps the child to develop a feeling for the wonder of growth, including his own beginnings.

"Where Do Babies Come From?"

A small child who asks where babies come from does not need a lecture. The simple answer, "Babies grow inside their mothers," may be quite enough for a three-year-old. Later he may ask if the baby grows in the mother's stomach. It can then be explained that the baby grows in a special little place made just for babies to grow in. The important thing is that the parents *want the child to know* what—and when—he wants to know. He will then feel free to come back again and again as his curiosity develops. By observation and alertness to his comments parents can sense whether their answers meet his needs.

The expected arrival of a baby brother or sister is a natural way to help a child understand that babies grow inside their mothers until they are big enough to be born. If no baby is expected, Mother and Father may talk together about a friend who is going to have a baby, mentioning how long the baby has been growing inside the mother and about when it will probably be born. He may not ask questions, but he can take in a surprising amount of information very early.

Edith Neisser in *Brothers and Sisters* has an excellent chapter on preparing the first child for the arrival of the second. Preparing the older child, psychologically, is far more important than the sex education aspects, but these can be easily included. Obviously it is not wise to ask him whether or not he would like a baby sister or brother if one is on the way. Any changes in his sleeping quarters necessitated by the arrival of another child should be made well in advance of its arrival, so that he does not feel shoved around by the newcomer. Letting him feel where the baby is growing, planning with him for the care of the baby—anything in fact that helps him feel "in on things"—tends to create better feeling for the new arrival.

Two sets of parents must have begun their children's sex education very early, for as their four- and five-year-olds were playing in the sandbox one day, a new seven-year-old in the neighborhood asked almost breathlessly, "Do you know where babies come from?" "Why, yes," said the five-year-old with worldly wisdom, "my mother told me that years ago." "Sure," declared the four-year-old, not to be outdone, "my mother told me that when I was on the way to the hospital to be born." While humorous, the children's answers are also symbolic. They learned so early and in so many ways that they did not remember learning.

"But my boy has never asked any questions. What can I do now?" a mother may ask.

That depends, of course, upon the child and upon his age, among other things. Children vary greatly in their interests, in what they notice, and in what they ask questions about. If he is only five or six, he may not have felt any need to ask. The mother might stimulate his interest in one of the ways suggested in the earlier discussion of children's questions. She might plan to visit a friend who is either expecting or who has a baby and, by prearrangement, talk with her about the baby in his presence. If he does not begin asking questions, then she might try asking him a few to find out what he already knows. Perhaps he has been getting his information from some older boy, and is embarrassed to ask. Something like this may be the case if the boy is eight or ten.

One of the easiest and best ways to go back and get caught up with children is to start off with some casual question, such as this, "When I was a little girl (or boy) I used to think that doctors brought babies in their little black bag. What did you think when you were younger?" This will normally free the child to tell the parent what he does know. This might be followed by another question, "When did you find out that babies grew inside their mothers?" Such questions may be helpful with almost any child five or six, or older. We must be shockproof and prepared to nod appreciatively at whatever they are willing to share with us. No clear blueprint exists for just what questions should be asked. The important thing is to be sensitive to the child's feelings and not move too fast. Some children may be uncomfortable and want to withdraw. If so, the parents will respect their feelings, and wait until later to make another opportunity for conversation. Other children seem glad to find that they can talk to their parents and, after a short period of adjustment to the new relationship, will bring up many questions they have suppressed.

The ideal to work toward is a warm, happy relationship, like that reported by one mother. Her eleven-year-old made some remark that shocked her as he was getting ready for bed one night. Her first impulse was to shame him for saying such a thing. Instead she asked him what it meant. He did not know. He had heard some older boys joking and laughing and had assumed that it was funny. "I didn't think he was old enough to know such things," she said, "but realizing that he was being exposed to it, I decided to talk things over with him." She told him about sex relations between men and women, putting major emphasis upon the sex relations between a man and woman who loved each other and who were married. He said little, but listened intently. The following night as she was tucking him in bed, he reached up and put his arms around her neck and whispered to her, "I'm glad you told me what you did last night. I feel lots better about it."

"How Does the Baby Get Out?"

A child probably wonders how a baby gets out of its mother, long before he finally is able to put the question into words. The parent may say, "When the tiny little baby is big enough to eat and breathe by itself it comes out of the mother through a special opening just for that purpose. You came out of your

Mommy in the same way." As the child grows, he may want more details. "When the baby is ready to be born, it begins to move out of the mother's body through her birth canal. This is an opening that leads from the place where the baby has been growing, to the outside. In most mother animals it is under their tail. In women this opening is down between the legs."

The idea of the elastic condition of the uterus and the vagina is important to convey. This seems to be most understandable to children in terms of a rubber balloon. "When the baby is tiny and just beginning to grow, the uterus is small like a balloon without any air in it. Then, as the baby grows, the uterus stretches just like a balloon when you blow it up. But the mother's uterus can stretch and stretch, and it never breaks. In the beginning it is about the size and shape of a pear, and just before the baby is born, it is almost as big as a watermelon. When the baby is ready to be born, the opening to the uterus stretches and allows the baby to pass out of the mother's body."

"Why Do Babies Have Fathers?"

When parents are asked why babies have fathers they may explain that all life begins with the union of male and female sex cells. There are always mother and father cats, cows, horses, fish, and other creatures. Children, too, come from the union of male and female sex cells.

Because many parents learned about human reproduction in ways emotionally charged with embarrassment, humor, or vulgarity, they are blocked in their efforts to tell their child what they know. It is especially important for fathers to learn a set of words to take the place of the four-letter ones most of them learned from older boys. Such words can hardly carry the right emotion—one of love and wonder. It is important to do this rewording because if a father does not know how to answer the question, "But how does the father's sex cell get into the mother?" he may really be afraid of all other questions. Once he has experimented with words and found a way to explain it with ease and good feelings, he will be more at ease with any other question relating to sex, for he knows he can handle it if it comes.

One marriage counselor, when asked by a mother in the group how he would explain intercourse, replied as follows: "Perhaps you could say something like this: When the father lies close to the mother, his penis fits naturally into her vagina or birth canal. The father's male sex cells go out of his body through his penis right into the mother's birth canal. The sex cells or sperms move upward in the canal, and if a mother's egg cell is there, one of the father's male cells joins with her egg cell and it begins to grow into a baby." This explanation may be used with a child from six or seven on.

One can comment further to the child about how human beings care for new babies. Fish merely lay their eggs in the bed of a stream and let them shift for themselves. But human mothers carry their growing baby inside until it is big enough to eat, drink, and breathe. When it is born, it needs care for a long time before it is able to take care of itself.

Explaining Menstruation to Children

What a mother tells her child about menstruation depends, of course, upon the age of the child, and the situation. If a young child should, for instance, see the mother wearing a pad, she might ask why the mother was wearing "that thing."

More important than the words she uses or the information offered is the way the mother herself feels about menstruation. "All women wear one of these a few days a month," she may say. That may be enough for the very young child. For a child eight or nine, one may say: "Once each month the mother's uterus or womb prepares to receive a fertilized cell or egg that could grow into a baby. But usually no fertilized egg comes, and so the little sac in which the baby would have grown had it arrived, is passed out of the body through the birth canal. Mother wears the pad to catch it."

If the child should see the blood, and be concerned lest Mother has been hurt, Mother can be reassuring, and add to her explanation something like this: "No, darling, I'm not hurt. When the little sac comes loose, the blood that has been stored as food for the new baby passes out too, and is caught by the pad. Next month the body will put some fresh blood there."

Later still, one would use the opportunity to prepare a little girl for menstruation. The range of age for normal first menstruation or monthly flow is very great—from nine years on, though thirteen is perhaps the average. Both sexes should know about menstruation from reliable sources. It would be ideal to show the film "The Story of Menstruation" to both boys and girls, and their parents, in the fifth grade at school. The film is very effective with its colored animated drawings and would be of equal interest to both boys and girls. So often boys find out about menstruation only through off-color or disparaging remarks of older boys. Girls often grow up having heard it referred to only as "the curse" or "the sickness." The film does much to prevent and correct these negative attitudes. It can profitably be shown to girls alone in the seventh grade.

Fascination with the Unusual

If natural curiosities are satisfied, children will be familiar with the basic facts of human reproduction and sexual intercourse between men and women before entering the sex-conscious, self-conscious early adolescent stage, roughly corresponding to the junior high school period—ages about twelve to fifteen.

During this stage, their curiosity turns to the unusual in human reproduction. For example, younger teen-agers are apt to come up with such questions as "How do you get twins?" "How do you get triplets?" "Siamese twins?"

The facts can be explained to them that twins occur about once in every eighty to ninety births, apparently run in families, and result from a variety of situations:

1. When two egg cells develop at the same time, probably one in each ovary, and both are fertilized, the twins are called "fraternal twins" and are no more alike than normal brothers and sisters. They may be of the same or different sex, may look alike or not, may have the same or different abilities.

2. "Identical twins," on the other hand, apparently result from a complete first division of one fertilized egg. One sperm fertilized it, and then the cell divided. Therefore the twins are always of the same sex, they look, and are, alike in almost every hereditary aspect, including abilities.

3. "Triplets" may be of several types. They may be
three "fraternal" beings from three eggs, or all
"identical," or one single and two identical twins.
It is not always easy to decide which is the case.
For a further discussion of this topic and numerous other inheritable features and characteristics
see Scheinfeld's *The New You and Heredity.*

Some other questions that are apt to catch a parent
off guard are "What is a Cesarean birth?" "What is a
'hermaphrodite'?" "Why does Johnny's penis look
different from mine?" "Why are some women's
breasts so big?"

By this time children have probably already discovered that parents are not the all-knowing and
omnipotent beings they once thought them to be. So
a parent gains, rather than loses, status, by saying, "I
don't know. Let's look it up." Then both are sure.

Or the parent might start out by asking some questions himself, such as "Why do you ask?" "In what
sense did you hear the term used?" "What do you
think it might mean?" "Why don't you look it up in
the dictionary?" There the teen-ager would find that
a "hermaphrodite" is "a human being or animal
combining characteristics of both sexes."

Again, "Why does Johnny's penis look different
from mine?" might well bring the counterquestion,
"Well, how does it look?" From the answer, it might

seem clear that it was not merely a matter of size, for instance, but that Johnny had, or had not, been circumcised. In this connection explanation could be made of why some parents have the child's foreskin clipped, and why others leave his penis as it was at birth. This might be explained in terms of religious or health reasons. An honest interest in the child's knowing the truth is the important thing. Parents who save themselves the problem of answering by such negative reactions as "I don't know, and please don't bother me with all those questions," slam the door in the child's face. If they do this often they may close the channels of communication between them and their child permanently.

The question, "Why are some women's breasts so big?" may have considerable importance attached to it, particularly if it comes from a girl. One girl asserted that she was never going to nurse her baby because she had once been told that a woman who had large and sagging breasts had nursed all her babies for a long time. When she was assured by the school nurse that with proper breast supports this need not occur, the girl felt differently.

Positive Attitudes Toward Sex in Marriage

It is not unusual for a young girl who has learned the facts of reproduction to say, "Why can't I have a baby now?" This is a fortunate question, for it gives an opportunity to relate intercourse and childbearing to marriage. By a series of questions she can be helped to realize why a baby needs two parents, and why it is important to grow all the way up, and have all the enjoyments of school, dating, and courtship before deciding whom she would want to be the father of her child.

It is important, too, to begin early to develop the idea that intercourse, like affection, is an expression of love. Some parents want to be sure their children have a knowledge of intercourse as an expression of affection, before they are exposed to the purely sexual treatment of it which they might get from other children. They often utilize some opportunity when they have been discussing reproduction to go on, perhaps, somewhat as follows:

"You know mothers and fathers don't have a baby every time they have intercourse together. Sometimes they have intercourse just because they enjoy it."

"Do you and Mommy do it?" the child may ask.

"Why, yes, of course. All married people do."

"But why?"

"Because it is very pleasant for them to lie close together with the father's penis in the mother's vagina. It is like kissing, only it makes them feel even more in love with each other than kissing does. It is part of what love is."

"How often do they do it?"

"Oh, whenever they both feel like it. Some do it often, others only occasionally."

"Could we see you and Mommy do it?"

"No, son, parents never allow children to see them."

"Why not?"

"Well, let's see. How would you feel to undress in the middle of the street?"

"Gee, I'd be embarrassed."

"Well, that's the way all married people feel about intercourse. It is something so intimate and lovely that they would not feel right to have anyone watch them. When you grow up and learn to love someone very much you will want to get married. And when you are married you will want to lie very close together and have intercourse. That is the way people are. You will feel that way too, when you are grown up."

The facts given are probably not the important things; it is the feelings parents share with their children that will determine their attitudes.

Some Helpful Ideas

"Marriage counselors make talking with children about sex sound so easy," some parents may feel. Certainly it will be easier for certain parents than for others because of background and attitudes, and also because people differ in the ease with which they express themselves. Here are some ideas that have helped others:

1. Parents need not wait for questions from the child to begin his sex education. If they are eager to share the wonder of life and living things with their child, they can build a rich background of casual experiences that both stimulate and satisfy curiosity.

2. Parents can become alert to words that convey ideas regarding sex meaningfully. They need not use scientific words unless these come easily. The important thing is for parents to decide what they want their child to know and how they want him to feel about it. By trying to put it in words and by asking one's mate how he or she would express it, parents gain confidence.

3. Words are not the only way of transmitting ideas. Calling attention to a picture in a magazine or book, or to something that is happening, or drawing a rough sketch, even a crude one, may be more meaningful than many words.

4. If a parent really listens to his children they will give him many opportunities to supplement with additional information, or to correct wrong impressions. When they ask a question they may want their parent's attention and love as much as the

answer to the question. The parent makes sure that he answers the child, not just his question.

5. A parent can profit from imagining the most difficult question a child could ask, or the most difficult situation that could arise, and then try to handle it. He mulls over the questions he would want to ask the child in order to get a clear picture before plunging in to explain. He tries to see how much of the answer he could draw from the child himself on the basis of their mutual past experiences and in what things the child has a vital interest to which the parent can relate new ideas.

6. A wise parent is prepared to say at times, "I don't know. Let's look it up." Even professionally trained people have to do that occasionally. In one large city a nurse spends almost all her time presenting to sixth graders the factual material dealing with human reproduction. Following each of her six illustrated talks, time is reserved for pupil questions. Although this nurse has had experience in answering, many times, most of the questions raised by the children, she occasionally gets one she cannot answer. "I don't know," she will say. "I'll look it up and give you the answer next time." Incidentally, the school and health authorities in that city think it is important for children to have information on human reproduction *before* they leave the elementary school, where sex

is not an important interest. They are not so be-
wildered, then, when they move into the junior
high school and find that sex *is* an important topic
of conversation there.

7. If enough parents request it, school personnel can
help. In that same city a man and a woman meet
with groups of boys and girls separately in junior
and senior high schools. Parents sign consent for
the youngsters to participate. These groups, too,
meet once a week for six weeks, being excused
from regular classes at that time. The first session
is an illustrated talk presenting the facts, appropriate to the age level. At the conclusion of each
meeting, time is taken to write out questions for
the next meeting. Many of the questions, the important ones, are the same in each group, and the
teachers become very competent at answering
them.

Keeping Channels Open Between Parents and Children

To help the child obtain accurate information
and a wholesome attitude parents must keep the
channels of communication open so that they know
his concerns, and can be sure he is building positive
attitudes. They can read together such books as *The
Wonderful Story of How You Were Born* by Gruenberg or *Growing Up* by DeSchweinitz.

Helpful books on sex education for home library shelves are an aid. One mother reported the front door bursting open and her ten-year-old son coming in, followed by several companions. "Here, I'll show you," he announced, going straight to the bookcase and taking out *Being Born* by Strain. He turned quickly to the desired page and showed them the picture, turning to his mother for confirmation of the disputed point. She had not been aware that her son had read the book, but apparently he had found it and learned to use it as a reference book. In books they can find some of the information they want when they need it.

Parents should encourage junior and senior high school libraries to have numerous books and pamphlets available, such as *Into Manhood* by Dickerson, *Teen Days* by Strain, and *The Facts of Life and Love for Teen-Agers* by Duvall. No child should be required to read them, but the books should be available to those who wish to read them.

Films which can be seen by both parents and children are useful to open or reopen discussion of sex information and attitudes. In some schools "Human Beginnings" is shown to first-grade mothers. Then, if the mothers desire it (and they usually do), the children are brought in and they see the film together. The children are not at all embarrassed and they talk and ask questions freely. "The Story of Menstruation" is good for fifth-grade boys and girls (some girls start then to menstruate) and to girls alone in the seventh grade. "Human Growth" was originally designed for seventh grade, but has been used more widely in the sixth grade, and even as far down as the fourth. After seeing a film, parents and youngsters have a natural basis for discussing it and for going far beyond.

These films are educationally excellent for children too. After seeing "Human Growth" a nine-year-old, whose parents had answered all his questions and had read books in this area with him, was asked whether he had learned anything new. "Well, I don't know whether I learned anything new—but it's sure a lot clearer." As the old Chinese proverb puts it, "One picture is worth a thousand words."

If the film is shown to the parents' group first, usually in a PTA meeting, and the overwhelming majority desire to see it with their children, it can be so arranged. If it is not feasible to show it during the regular class program when they are accustomed to seeing educational films, it can be run off after hours. Unsigned questionnaires collected from the parents give a more accurate picture of whether or not they wish their children to see the film. Those opposed usually speak out against it. Those who approve, often just listen—and then vote favorably if they have a chance.

But more than buying books or seeing films is needed to keep the channels open. As they approach their teens, boys in particular talk openly about sex with other boys in a stimulating manner. They may bring home jokes that got a laugh and repeat them without really understanding them. A few questions can reveal these sources of information and not only enable parents to help their children understand new terms but to see the wisdom of not repeating jokes which they do not understand or which might offend others. If parents are not shockproof, or if they reprimand their boys, they may build a barrier against further communication. If they can laugh with the boys at the really funny jokes—and there are many humorous aspects of sex—and ask rather pointedly, "What's funny about that?" when a joke is sprung that is neither funny nor nice, parents can help them learn to discriminate—and still keep the channels open so that they may know what their children are being exposed to. Much laughing and joking about sex is a form of tension release, a natural reaction to embarrassment. If wholesome, discriminating attitudes are thus developed, children will have less need to listen to and tell "sexy" stories.

Most important of all in stimulating the free flow of ideas between parents and children is the availability of parents for leisurely talk. Often a number of superficial interests have to be talked out before the real problem will come to the surface. Sitting quietly on the edge of a child's bed, rubbing his back gently, listening with interest and understanding makes it easier for him to share his concerns, or to raise questions that may come to mind.

Availability and prying are very different things, however, and children sense the difference. As they approach adolescence, parents should not expect their children to want to share everything with them and should not be hurt if they turn elsewhere for advice. As one young girl put it, when she was asked if she had talked to her mother, "I already know what my mother would say; I want to know what *you* think." Older friends and other adults in the community can be an invaluable resource in helping youth to get a sound basis for the judgments they will want to make for themselves.

CHAPTER 3

Modesty Develops in Time

Modesty is defined as ". . . held back by a sense of what is fitting and proper . . . decent; not calling attention to one's body." Parents want their children to have this sense of fitness and decency, but they want it rooted in respect for themselves and their bodies, and in consideration for the feelings of others—not in a false and inhibiting fear.

Why are parents in such a hurry to make children self-conscious about their bodies? Are they afraid the next generation will grow up to be nudists unless they are taught that it is not nice to expose the body? (Actually nudists are often people who may be openly and violently rebelling against an overly modest upbringing.) Are people afraid of the criticism of neighbors or friends? They feed their children Vitamin D to make up for the sun's rays they don't get because they are afraid to let them expose the entire body to the sun when they can, in the back yard, or in a wading pool in the park.

A group of small children, aged about three to six, were having a wonderful time running and splashing in a shallow pool in a public park. In the excitement, the tiny swimming suit of one toddler came down. He stepped out of it and went merrily on. Other youngsters noticed him and proceeded to shed their swimming and sun suits too. They had a wonderful time until one of the mothers became aware of what had happened. She dashed to the edge of the pool, called her child, ordered him to bring his little swim suit, put it on him bruskly, and marched him off with the reproach, "You were a *very* bad boy!" Why was he bad?

A similar incident occurred at the beach recently. The mother of the child who had shed his suit smiled, but went to him and asked him to bring his suit to her. She helped him slip it on, saying casually, "We keep our suit on when we swim here." She did not want her child to make others uncomfortable, nor to become uncomfortable himself if he were to discover a little later that he was an object of curiosity to others.

How can parents help their children to develop more naturally healthy attitudes toward their own and others' bodies, their own and the other sex? Can this be done without making them insensitive to the attitudes of others or giving them a desire to shock the oversensitive person, just to show how free they are?

First, Acceptance of One's Own Body

Self-acceptance begins with the acceptance of one's own body and its normal functions. Unconscious self-rejection, which may masquerade later in life as a need to impress others (really an attempt to impress oneself) may begin with parental rejection of the basic eliminative functions of the child—making him feel that bowel movements are "dirty" and wetting is "bad." No group tries so hard as middle-class Americans to rush its children into toilet training. Why? And what is the effect of making them feel guilty or "dirty" about their normal functions? Does it speed up toilet training? Here the answer is definitely "NO." Control is determined by nerve maturation, not by parental pressure.

The child will want to control his functions, when he is able. Best results are obtained by cheerfully praising *his* achievement as he improves. Forcing often develops hostilities so that the child may continue to punish a parent for years. Acceptance of him, including his bowel movements and wet panties, make it easier for him to accept himself, and others.

"Aren't our bodies wonderful," a mother can comment as she bathes her child. He, or she, will enjoy hearing it, and it will help to build good feeling about his own body. The mother can enjoy with him his good feeling as he soaks in a warm bath, lies in the sun at the beach, or steps out of a cold shower. "Doesn't it feel good," she can suggest as she gives him an alcohol rub, or tucks him into a comfortable bed when he is tired and sleepy.

Has there been, perhaps, too much emphasis upon the "sins of the flesh" and not enough upon the "sins against the flesh?" Did not God create these bodies with all their response patterns, each with a vital function in life? If eating were not pleasurable more people would suffer from malnutrition. If sex were not pleasurable fewer men would be willing to assume the responsibility that goes with marriage and the support of a wife and children. Even within marriage itself, men and women have been made to feel a little guilty in finding bodily pleasure in sexual gratification—although that very gratification may have given them warmer feelings for each other and strengthened their marriage.

Children, as they grow up, are going to be exposed in varying degree to the bodies of the other sex. Assuredly some of the individuals who call their attention to exposed bodies, or who expose their own, are not going to have the attitudes parents want their children to "catch." If wholesome attitudes toward the human body can be developed early, then instead of "getting a kick" out of the off-color remarks they will hear about a dancer, someone's pin-up girls, or the suggestive figures on the calendar in the local garage, their reaction may well be, "What's so funny about that?" even if they don't say so audibly.

Parents can comment on the beautiful bodies of athletes, dancers, and models as they appear on the cover or in the ads of the magazines that come into the home. The children are going to notice them, because they are interested in bodies—their own and others. Or when art galleries and parks are visited, there is opportunity to comment on the beauty of the human body as portrayed in sculpture and painting, with attention called to the beauty, strength, and life the artist has captured in bronze or stone, or on canvas.

How Nudist the Family?

There seems to be general agreement that it is good to bathe young children of the family together, regardless of sex. If this is done from the beginning the children attach no particular concern to the sex organs, yet they become familiar with the genital organs of the other sex. Any curiosity is satisfied as it develops. "That is fine for small children, but how long is it safe to continue this practice?"

someone may ask. One parent presented an interest-ing report on this score:

"I watched modesty develop over the years. We used to put our three children in the tub together and they always had a wonderful time soaking, swim-ming, and even splashing gently. They took turns washing each other's back, and seemed to be entirely unsex-conscious. We wondered how long we should continue the practice and decided we would let it go along until we saw some evidence that it was time to stop it. We hated to interfere when they seemed to enjoy it so much.

"One night when the oldest youngster was about eight, she announced that it was getting too crowded to bathe with the other kids and that she was going to bathe alone after that. She did. Maybe it was in part crowding, and in part an unrecognized self-con-sciousness. The other two continued bathing together for a couple of years. Gradually the boy, who was the older, began to keep a washcloth over his penis most of the time, but they continued to have fun bathing together. After a few months, the girl seemed to imi-tate him, for she began to keep a washcloth over her vulva, too. Then at about the same age at which his older sister had deserted the group, the boy began locking the door to the bathroom when he went in to bathe. I'm convinced that all three of these children just developed a sort of natural modesty when they were about eight, and felt more comfortable bathing alone."

Many parents with similar attitudes have had similar experiences. Does modesty have to be "taught"— or is it an aspect of a growing self-consciousness that will develop gradually and naturally on the part of the child without intervention from the parents?

And what about dressing, and unlocked doors of bedrooms and bathrooms? It is not to be assumed that all parents can, or should, allow complete freedom. To go beyond what is "comfortable" for them because they thought they should, would be to confuse the child. Many parents do not deliberately "expose" themselves to their children; nor, on the other hand, do they "make something of it" by ordering children out of their bedroom when they want to get dressed. Children soon pay little attention to casual exposure if they are brought up in such an environment. It is common courtesy that if a bathroom or bedroom door is closed, anyone desiring to enter knocks and awaits permission before entering. A knock may sometimes bring a cheery "Come in"; at other times, a question, "Who is it?" If it is Daddy needing to shave, the "Come on in" signal may be given. If it is one of the other children, the response may be, "I'm taking a bath; you'll have to wait." The desire for privacy varies with individuals and with age. It should be respected.

When Different Sexes Share a Room

A common problem in many families where a growing family begins to "bulge" in what were, when the children were young, quite adequate quarters, is the age at which boys and girls should no longer share a room. Most parents now recognize that it is important for adolescents to have a room of their own, if this is possible. In any case, no one would expect adolescents of different sexes to share a room. But just where does the transition come?

Again, there is no one answer. And again, the determining factor may be the way the parents and children feel about it. When the parents begin to feel uncomfortable, it would be surprising if they did not transmit that feeling to the children. On the other hand, sometimes children adjust so easily that parent's concerns are relieved. One couple reported taking a small three-bedroom cottage at the beach for the summer. They had assumed that the nine-year-old girl would have the small single room, and the boys would share the larger bedroom with its double-decker. To their surprise, the children had it all worked out before the parents could get the car unloaded and have a hand in the decision. The younger girl did not want to sleep alone in the small room, but preferred to sleep in the top bunk, sharing the room with the younger of the two boys, as they had done several years before. The nine- and twelve-year-olds got along congenially for the most part, and the fifteen-year-old boy enjoyed the privilege of later hours and a room of his own.

There was no self-consciousness from seeing each other in pajamas—they had always done that. When it came time to dress, one headed for the bathroom, locked the door, and changed there. The other then changed in the locked bedroom. It was common to hear one tell the other, "Scram, I want to get dressed." There was nothing to indicate that there was any problem at all, though the awareness that this arrangement was temporary may have been a factor.

A few weeks before they were to leave, the two sharing the room had a scrap about something outside and entirely irrelevant to their sleeping quarters. The girl asked the older brother to share the bedroom for the remaining time. He surprised everyone, apparently, by readily agreeing. Again there was the careful respect of the other's privacy—knocking on closed doors before entering, and no apparent strain of any kind. Both parents agreed that the children were more comfortable about the arrangement than they were, although neither child would have accepted it as a permanent arrangement. But it does show again, that probably children, brought up with a minimum of forced and unnatural "modesty" have a comfortable and workable modesty that far surpasses in adjustability anything known or permitted in previous generations.

That attitudes are "built in" during early childhood is perfectly obvious to anyone who studies the behavior of children. When children come to nursery school for the first time, they are often reluctant to go to the toilet with other children of even the same sex. But after a few exposures to children of both sexes sharing toilet facilities, they become as unselfconscious as the rest.

One parent reported a most amusing, but revealing, neighborhood taboo, probably innocently initiated by some parent. This father reported being amused by an expressed concern of his children that no other child must "see my behiney." "One morning," he said, "the children were dressing in the front room when the door burst open and several neighborhood children came in. One of my children was completely naked, the other had on only a little shirt. Both quickly backed to the wall and around the room and out the door into the hall, then dashed for their bedroom. The other children must not see their 'behiney.' The fact that their genitals were completely exposed seemed of no concern to them at all."

Children learn to feel about their bodies the way they are taught to feel by their parents, or by other children's parents, through their children. Young children are not self-conscious about their bodies. It was perfectly natural for a little girl who was breathlessly told by her mother as the doorbell rang, "Don't let Mrs. Jones see you in that dirty nightgown," to disappear and return a minute later minus the "dirty nightgown."

In Summary

America is a land of contradictions as far as modesty is concerned. In some ways, we still carry in our nerve endings many of the inhibitions that have come down from overly modest Puritan ancestors. In other ways we are at the mercy of "ad men" who have discovered that sex is the number one attention-getting device in America today.

America has moved in one lifetime from the complete covering of the body of women to the Bikini bathing suit. Women wear strapless formals with plunging necklines, go to the supermarkets in shorts and bras but are horrified to see a three-year-old urinating unself-consciously in the middle of the front lawn. One such youngster challenged this confusion when he said, "You put the doggie out, and you make me come in. Why?" Are we clear that this is a matter of hygienic sanitation and consideration for other people's feelings—and can we make that clear to a three-year-old instead of making him think it is "bad" in itself?

Attitudes can and do change. A young college president of thirty years ago, visiting the women's gym to see about some needed equipment, blushed when the woman physical education instructor, dressed in middy blouse, baggy black bloomers, black stockings, and tennis shoes, greeted him in the hall. Twenty-five years—and a generation of change—later, he watched the Modern Dance class going through intricate and graceful movements during May Day dances on the lawn and commented appreciatively to some of his faculty colleagues, "How graceful and beautiful is the human body!" Attitudes are changing. "Be not the first by whom the new is tried, nor yet the last to lay the old aside" is probably still comfortable advice for most of us. The normal youngster gradually develops an awareness of what constitutes good taste in terms of parental and group judgments. He becomes conscious of the way his behavior affects other people by the way in which they respond to it.

CHAPTER 4

Love-Sex Feelings in the Early Years

If parents want their children to love life and love other people they must make it possible for them to experience such feeling at all ages, but particularly during the early years. Children respond readily to their environment, and lovable parents can tip the scales in the right direction.

Most people have warm feeling for a cooing infant, and he responds to them; but it is not easy for parents to love children who awaken them early in the morning or refuse to eat their cereal. Children can be decidedly irritating at three, when they say "no" to every request as they discover for the first time that they have a mind of their own; or at four, when they go through that finicky stage when they want only what they want, when they want it. At times they may threaten one's sense of authority, as a three-year-old did when he climbed to the very top of the jungle gym in the park and refused to come down until he was ready to do so. Fortunately, after her first moment of panic at seeing him there, the mother felt with him the glorious thrill of adventure and achievement and allowed him to remain a few minutes, until his need for adventure and ego satisfaction were temporarily satiated and his need for security brought him down.

No parents feel love for their children at all times. One mother who had been very angry at her four-year-old, commented afterwards, "I love you, but I sometimes get angry at what you do." "No, Mommy," corrected the six-year-old brother who had observed the situation, "you didn't love Karin when you were mad at her." The mother laughed as she related the incident. "He was right, I didn't. We can fool ourselves, but we can't fool children, can we?"

Why should we need to fool ourselves? Why can we not admit that it is natural to feel intense dislike as well as love? As long as it is *usually* love, the child can take occasional outbursts in stride. So can parents, for there will be times when their children may even dislike them, too. To feel strongly *toward* someone means that we may also feel strongly *against* that person when, as is inevitable at times, he lets us down.

What Is Love?

"Oh, I love your new car," a woman tells a neighbor as she looks appreciatively at the beautiful three-color creation he has just purchased.

"I just love strawberry shortcake," exclaims Johnny as his mother brings in a delicious dessert.

"I love Billy," a first grader tells her mother of the little boy who has let her ride his pony.

"I love you, darling; will you marry me?" whispers the young man to the even younger girl of his dreams.

"I love my husband, and I'm sure he loves me," a middle-aged woman replies to her sister, who cannot understand why she doesn't leave her husband, since he has had an affair with another woman.

"I love you, darling," Daddy tells his little son as he tucks him in bed and kisses him on the forehead.

"I love to do things for my family," a mother tells her happy little brood sincerely, for it makes her happy to see them so happy.

Obviously the word has a somewhat different meaning in each case. But one thing is common to all; something makes someone feel good inside. Many things make for good feeling. We feel good when our basic needs for love, for security, for a sense of personal worth and achievement are satisfied; and we love the people that satisfy these needs. Body feelings are good; the child loves the people who satisfy his need for food when he is hungry, a soft bed when he is sleepy, a warm bath that relaxes him. He also loves the feel of his big toe, his penis, or his soft tender skin.

Early Experiences Toward Good Feelings

One of the earliest cycles of good feeling is set up when a mother nurses and cuddles her newborn infant. In the succeeding months a host of pleasant sensations—the delightful warmth of his bath, the warm rays of the sun upon his bare skin, those spoonfuls of new taste delights, the cup of milk he is able to bring to his lips with his own hands— all these sensations become associated with the woman whose cheerful chatter and soft lullaby give him a sense of well-being.

Such joys, however, are not limited to mothers. A mother was holding her one-year-old daughter when the father's step sounded at the front door. "Daddy!" Mother's single word changed a relaxed and happy baby into an excited and alert little nymph. Toddling as fast as her wobbly little legs could carry her, she headed for her Daddy with a beaming smile, eyes wide with excitement, and arms outstretched. Daddy dropped down onto one knee and they enfolded each other in a delightful embrace.

She is already off to a good start in her feeling about men, because she *loves* her Daddy.

Her response did not suddenly happen. Month after month Daddy had played with her, smiled at her, cuddled her, and, as he had had opportunity, bathed her, fed her, put her to bed, and taken her up. And day after day, a mother who understood that love was not limited, not indivisible, but potentially limitless and overflowing, had triggered with that one magic word, "Daddy," the reception which produced so much good feeling in all three.

It takes time, appreciation and shared enjoyment to earn the love of children. Too many modern parents are too busy, too hurried, too tired at the end of a hectic day to give their children the affection and undivided attention they seek. When parents act as though the job, golf, the newspaper, bridge, or the house were more important than their children, they damage their children's basic feelings of personal worth upon which future ambition, self-confidence, and personal courage depend.

Fortunately, it is never too late to change. One father told of realizing that he and his sixteen-year-old son were almost strangers. He had been so busy building up an investment business that he had given little time or thought to his adolescent boy. The years slipped by while he seldom saw his son except at dinner, and then they seemed to have nothing to say to each other. When he stopped to analyze what had happened, he determined to change their relationship. But how?

"My son gave me a clue," the father said, "when he mentioned that one of his pals was going fishing at a distant lake. A few questions brought out the fact that the boy went with his dad regularly and had a wonderful time."

"Why don't we get some fishing tackle and go too?" the father had said almost impulsively. A great smile broke over his son's face, "Gee, Dad, I didn't know you liked to fish!"

"Sure, I do. I guess I've been too busy to go," Father replied. "But Jim Hurley has joined my staff now and is going to take over a lot of my responsibilities, so I can get away more. If you'll help me pick out some gear, I'd love to go with you."

He continued, telling in great detail how he and his son had gone fishing again and again during the years that followed, culminating in a month-long hiking and fishing trip into the back country of California's High Sierras. "He nearly killed me off that summer hiking me over those mountain passes, but it was worth it. I won back my boy. It was the best investment I ever made." As he spoke the tears filled his eyes and he was not ashamed; for, a few days before, he had received a telegram from the War Department which began, "We regret to inform you. . . ." His son had been one of those young fliers who had given their all for their country.

This is not to imply that every father ought to take his son fishing! In this case both loved to fish and it became a bond of togetherness. Had they not enjoyed fishing, *and each other,* the results would not have been satisfying to either one. For another father and son it might be baseball or boating; for another, photography or building a new room on the house. For still others, it might be music, gardening, or collecting rocks. Where there is good feeling, there will be a desire on the part of each to share with the other. It is the desire for togetherness that makes both child and parent more sensitive to what gives joy to the other. As each gives, he experiences not only the satisfactions of giving, but of *sharing*—the most human, and therefore the most loving, of all experiences.

Good feeling for other children is important too. In *Brothers and Sisters,* Edith Neisser gives numerous suggestions for helping brothers and sisters live more happily together. Preparing the oldest child for the jolt of yielding the center of the stage to another, or at least sharing it; learning to accept the inevitable rivalry and jealousy of children for their parents' love and time; finding ways of slowly and patiently welding a group of prima donnas into a family—these are important tasks in the development of good feelings toward others. For feeling tones are fashioned to a considerable degree in the families in which we grow up.

Fortunate indeed is the child who has the opportunity to care for younger children. Often this relationship is most rewarding when the children cared for are not brothers and sisters but other small children. Of course, the care of younger brothers and sisters *may* become an unpleasant chore, which creates more resentment than good feeling. But, if parents are alert to encourage and reward with praise and privileges the voluntary acceptance of responsibility for younger children, and if they try to create an atmosphere of good family fun and exciting good times together, the good feelings which are generated within the family circle are among the most vital and lasting. For all children, but for the oldest and only child particularly, nursery school or a co-operative play group may prove of great value. Katharine Whiteside Taylor in her *Parent Co-operative Nursery Schools* gives a wealth of insight into the values and techniques of co-operative play groups, as does Katherine Read in *The Nursery School,* for the more formally operated nursery school.

Playmates of the other sex during the early years help to develop good feeling toward the other sex from the beginning. One of the greatest changes during our generation is that fewer and fewer fathers are saying, "Now look, Johnny, I don't want you to be a sissy and play with the girls. Play with boys, and be a real boy."

The result of this freedom we grant to children to choose their own playmates is that they play together "unsex-consciously" during the early years. By the time they start to school, their capacity to feel and express affection is apt to bring on a rash of first-grade crushes. "What should we do about these first-grade romances?" teachers often ask anxiously. "Terry goes around trying to kiss all the girls," or "Billy keeps trying to kiss Mary, and she gets very cross with him." Teachers can usually be encouraged to observe this behavior but to interfere as little as possible. In the classroom, of course, they should stop behavior which interferes with the class or annoys other children—just as they would any other undesirable behavior. They should not, however, say, "Boys who are little gentlemen don't try to kiss little girls," or similar remarks—and neither should parents.

It seems clear that children show amazing insight in choosing, as friends, children who meet their dominant need at a particular time. A new child entering a school may be taken under the wing of the class bully whom few of the other children like; they may become bosom pals. The bully needs a friend; and the new child needs, because of his insecurity in the new situation, to be near someone who is strong and who will protect him. It pleases him to have the dominant member choose him as a friend—and vice versa. After his self-confidence in the situation is developed, he may come to resent the dominant ways of the other and choose another friend, who meets a new need. Encouraging children in their friendships by accepting all their friends, and expecting changes in friends as natural seems the best policy.

Playing with dolls has long served to nurture the development of good feeling toward something outside the self. Dolls, like so many other interests which "catch on" and continue generation after generation, do so because they serve some basic human needs. Every human being needs to love and be loved. In addition, we all need to have a sense of power. Because of their own helplessness, children need to have *power over* something in order to develop a sense of adequacy and overcome their feelings of inferiority to the older children and adults who surround them. They attempt to exercise *power over* their parents, and it is undoubtedly good to give in to some of these demands. Parents spoil their children only when they give in to unreasonable demands as well as reasonable ones lest they lose their children's love. A firm "No," with affection, helps children learn that it is better to have power *with people* and power *over things.*

Dolls serve such a function; they do not resist or resent what children do to them. The child may project good feeling upon his dolls and assume that they feel the same way about him. The need to love and feel loved, and the need to have *power over* things can thus be satisfied, and both are blended in happy play with dolls.

Boys as well as girls profit from play with dolls and enjoy doing so if they are not made to feel that it is unmanly. Having big "Mother" and "Daddy" dolls, and smaller dolls to parallel his family group, offers much opportunity for the child to play out or work off any unpleasant feelings he may have toward other members of the family. Psychologists use dolls in play therapy to allow just such ventilation of unconscious hostilities. But one does not have to be a psychologist to get the point when the father doll is always cross with his children, the mama doll is always telling her children to run out and play so that she can get her work done, the baby brother doll is wrapped up, placed in a shoebox, and "buried" in the flower bed. We can learn much from watching this play. And when the papa and mama dolls often love their doll children, parents may feel more securely that their children are really learning from them to be good "papas and mamas."

How Pets Can Help

Pets are a bother, of course, at times, but well worth the effort if not introduced too soon, before the children—or the parents—are really ready for them.

"I'd rather have Smoky than a thousand dollars!" said Tim feelingly, petting the head of his beloved dog. And he meant it. Smoky was just dog, but what a dog! For warm responsiveness and affection he would be hard to match. Perhaps that accounted in part for the willingness of the children to feed him, to keep him clean and brushed, to train him. But the children's ages also played a part, as did their previous experience in caring for a cat. The cat had been easier to housebreak and more capable of looking out for itself.

Children must have achieved considerable competence in caring for themselves before they are capable of assuming full responsibility for pets. An important part of love is the desire to *care for* anyone or anything that we *care about*. But it is one thing for a child under ten or eleven to help care for a family pet, and quite another if a parent has unrealistic expectations about the amount of responsibility the child is able to assume. In the latter case, the friction generated by forcing him to care for the pet may well result in his soon not caring about it,

especially if parents exasperatedly nag instead of re-
minding the child of the pet's needs in a thoughtful
way. If the parents have too much at stake financially
in the pet, emotion may run high as they seek to
protect their investment.

Female pets have special advantages. They not
only offer a wonderful stimulus to education regarding physical reproduction but, perhaps even more
important, give children a good feeling about the
"mothering" process. When a growing pet first comes
into heat, the co-operation of the children can be
enlisted in preventing it from mating before fully
grown. One child, taking her young cat out for
fresh air, was heard to tell the other neighborhood
children in a very wholesome way, "I have to be
careful of Taffy. That old tomcat wants to mate with
her, but she isn't big enough. We want her to be
grown all the way up before she has babies." The
idea that it is good to be grown all the way up before
mating should be a good one to plant in the minds
of all children.

Five-year-old Janie stood silently watching the
birth of a tiny coal black kitten. Then she looked up
with shining eyes. "Midnight *loves* her kitten! She's
just licking it all over!" Soon there were three little
kittens, their bodies close against the warmth of the
mother. Sue, eleven, was also watching. She, too,
looked up with delight. "Midnight's purring. She's

so happy!" She was lost in wonder that after all these weeks of waiting, this could really be happening. "It's a miracle!" she exclaimed softly.

Sue did not need to be urged to get some milk for Midnight, to be sure that her pet had food and water close at hand and a box of sand as well. Much to her mother's surprise, she laid out her sleeping bag on the attic floor, preparing to spend the night close to the box which housed the foursome. "This must have been quite a strain on Midnight," she commented to her mother. "No, I don't think it was," her mother replied, "Midnight didn't seem at all disturbed. She said 'Meow,' but more as if she wanted us to notice her kittens than as if in pain."

The emotional impact on all the children who were close to this birth experience was unquestionably positive. Reverence for the mystery of life, plus warm, outgoing good feeling, was registered in their faces and in their behavior as well as in their words.

Sue's grace at dinner that evening was a fitting climax. ". . . Thank you for all the miracles you set before us. Help us to realize all of them!"

Now Sue knew quite a lot about reproduction from wide experience with pets, ranging from guppies and hamsters to dogs and horses. She had watched rabbits mate and had witnessed the birth of little pigs. She had been well aware of the period when Midnight had been in heat and of the many Toms who came to call. She had wondered which one would prove to be the father. She had seen the film "Human Growth" and had talked freely with her parents about sex. Yet this range of experience, this knowledge, did not detract from the wonder and mystery of new life coming into being. To have awareness of miracles or the potentials for miracles that lie all about us—what wouldn't such awareness do to our human relationships!

Schools can also help in the early elementary grades by having pets in the classroom. One woman who had developed good feelings about sex in her own children, had her husband take the rabbit hutch to school. The children were much interested in the mother rabbit, and in knowing that there were little baby rabbits growing inside the mother. The date of expected arrival was red-lettered on the calendar, and each morning a day was checked off. A different child daily was privileged to bring lettuce leaves, carrots, and potato peelings for the rabbit. There was much excitement when the babies arrived, and a few children at a time had a chance to see how tiny and hairless they were. Every few days the youngsters were allowed to see how much they had grown. Finally the little bunnies came out of the nest and were a constant source of wonder and enjoyment to the children. Just before they were taken back home, one seven-year-old looked up from watching the rabbits and said, almost in a reverent whisper, "Isn't it wonderful?" "The reaction of that one child alone made all the effort undergone worth while," the teacher commented to an associate.

Alerting Without Frightening Children

In Los Angeles an old man who is slowly losing his mental faculties molests a six-year-old girl, and then kills her in the fear that she will tell and he will be punished. In the Middle West, an emotionally unbalanced young man abducts, rapes, and murders a little girl. In New Hampshire a seventeen-year-old boy, baby sitting, molests and then chokes to death a four-year-old girl when she says she will tell her mother.

Reading of these incidents in the paper, some parents are afraid for their little girls. They lose perspective and forget that the press has a special interest in the sensational. They do not stop to think that on the same day on which these incidents happened—isolated incidents, separated by several years and several thousand miles—ten million American youngsters lived through a happy and uneventful day. That fact is not "news."

In only one of the cases just mentioned was there any negligence on the part of the parents. The parents of the first little girl knew that on several occasions the old man had shown his genitals to children in the park. The children, more amused than frightened, had run home and told their parents. The parents had been concerned, but they had not wanted to "make trouble" for the old man, so they had not reported the incidents to the police. Had they done so, and had the police of that city had at their disposal a psychiatrist or clinical psychologist to examine the old man and determine whether or not he was "dangerous," the tragedy, in all probability, would not have happened.

What is the answer? Certainly not an overdose of fear of "strangers." For none of these killers were strangers. The children knew them, and so did the parents. To build up a fear of strangers is to isolate children in a world of dangerous people, for if they are afraid to make friends, most of the people they see will be "dangerous strangers." That is too high a price to pay.

In contrast, consider the fourth grader who was somewhat anxious about going off to school the first day after her parents moved to what was to her a new and strange community. Her parents assured her that she would find the children and teachers as friendly as back home. The mother, in turn, began to worry when the child did not return from school at the expected hour. When she appeared, an hour later, with a new little friend, mother was torn between the desires to hug her and to spank her. Fortunately the hug won out. The child had stopped at the home of her new-found friend who lived just a block away. Later she told her mother that Susan's mommy and daddy were very nice. "You know, Mommy, I think there are nice people everywhere. Anywhere we go, we can always find friends." What a wonderful attitude of expectancy! And because she expects people to be friendly, they usually will be.

And yet, there are a few mentally ill or sexually perverted people. How can children be alerted to them without undue alarm?

The first step parents can take is to make it easy for children to tell them anything that happens without fearing that their parents will become excited and make more of it than is justified or overreact by clamping more controls on them. If parents encourage children to think that their teachers, policemen, and bus drivers are their friends and want to protect them, they will feel free to report to a teacher any incident that has happened on the way to school, or to report to the officer directing traffic at the school anything that seems unusual. Parents can encourage them to let the adults decide whether it is anything that needs investigation.

Second, parents can let children know their confidence is respected. Many children have heard their parents laughingly tell neighbors or friends some concern they have shared with their parents as confidential. This makes them reluctant later to tell their parents about other troubles.

Naturally, children must be taught not to accept candy or free rides from strangers. This is something that just is not done. And parents must teach them that if anything happens involving a car, they are to be alert to notice what color and make the car is, and if possible jot down the license. If they cannot get the whole number, it helps to be sure of the last three figures. If they have no pencil, they can use their fingers to write the number in the dust on a parked car, or on anything else on which they can make a mark.

One way that some parents have found helpful is to utilize certain incidents that are reported in the newspaper. For example, in Seattle a "nice man" picked up a little brother and sister walking home from school. On the way, he offered to buy them some candy. He went into a drugstore, held it up, and then dashed back to the car, and made his getaway. The owner of the store and a nearby policeman, seeing the children in the car, held their fire. One family discussed this at the dinner table. Their children saw what might have happened if the policeman had not seen the little children in the car, or if the man had decided to kidnap them instead of putting them out of the car a few blocks away, as he did. By discussing incidents that actually happen, our approach can be more natural.

Parents might even feel it wise to discuss some incidents of sex molestation with their children. They can help them to understand that there are a few older boys or men who do not have the ability to control their behavior the way most men do. These men usually start out quite innocently by being nice, and then want to see or play with the child's genitals. Children must be taught that such men are not normal and that they must get away from them as soon as they can.

Sometimes these incidents start in theaters. Such a man moves from his seat and sits down next to a girl who is alone. He is nice and friendly, offers her candy, and may then begin by just letting his leg press against hers. If she does not move away, he soon follows with his hand, and begins to rub her leg. After a while he may suggest that she go somewhere with him after leaving the theater.

It is best, of course, for girls to attend theaters in pairs or groups. If a girl does have to go alone, she should be reminded by her parents to sit down by another woman or a couple—not by herself. If a man should sit down next to her when there are other vacant seats around, she might be on guard. If he tries to sit very close to her, she should move to another seat, telling the usher quietly that she thinks the man is trying to get fresh. The usher will then keep an eye on the man. After several such incidents, the management usually notifies the police. The man is then picked up for questioning, and his record is checked. If he is in the clear, he will normally be released with a stern warning as to the consequences. It is very difficult to convict anyone on children's evidence. The important effect of such immediate action by the child is that it prevents anything serious from happening to her, and that a resulting "brush with the law" may well frighten and restrain such an unstable person. He may have drifted into this type of sexually stimulating behavior without realizing how serious it might become. Police often withhold charges if the individual reports to the nearest Mental Hygiene Clinic to get help on a problem that could well land him in jail. This treatment of avoidance and reporting has also proved effective in the case of "queer" adults who have drifted into homosexual relations with young boys without realizing that this makes them liable to criminal charges. People fear to report such cases, because of the harsh punishment the law may inflict. When people feel reasonably sure that the police and the courts will handle such individuals as mentally sick persons in need of treatment rather than as criminals deserving punishment, they will much more readily report such questionable behavior.

If children are brought up to be self-confident and resourceful, and are given a good sex education, they may well react as an eleven-year-old girl did when a man sat down next to her on a bus, tried to be friendly, and then to "feel her." "What did you do?" her mother asked her as calmly as she could when the girl told her. "I told the man that wasn't nice, and I got up and moved to another seat." "Children can really look out for themselves pretty well, can't they, if we give them a real respect for themselves and for sex," the mother concluded in telling of the incident.

In a case reported by *Child-Family Digest* (March, 1955, page 60), a seven-year-old girl marched into the house and told her mother a boy in his early teens had "tried to rub me." The mother was naturally agitated, but she asked the child what she did. "Why, I pushed him away, of course! I told him those parts were made for other things when I'm a big lady. He won't try *that* again." The author applauded the little girl's handling of the situation, and the wholesome sex education her parents must have given her. "If she had not known why she was made as she was, might she not have been more willing to join in the experiment?"

Prevention is, of course, the best policy. But if

sex molestation should happen, the parents' attitude will determine largely whether it is to have a lasting harmful effect or whether it is another "incident" of childhood. Trying to make neither too much, nor too little, of it, should be the goal. Asking questions which show the child their interest and understanding, and which at the same time give the youngster a chance to talk out her feelings seems to be the best course. "How did you feel . . ." questions encourage the child to express real feelings. If the child is seriously disturbed, if she has nightmares, or shows other serious symptoms, the minister or family doctor can probably suggest a trained counselor to help the parents reduce for the child the fears and anxieties the incident may have caused, and thus prevent any permanent after-effects.

"I don't know why people are so worried about today's youth," said one mother whose daughter had been followed by a mentally retarded man. "They are so clear-eyed about things. They seem to understand that people are different and to take them in stride."

How Love Drives Out Fear

Because reaching out expectantly to people so often gives a good feeling to all concerned, one might well ask why there is not more love and less hate and suspicion in the world. Does not a partial answer lie in the fears that have been built into our responses as we have grown up?

Fear and love are contradictory emotions. Fear stimulates emergency flight or fight reactions, short-circuiting the thinking areas of the brain. The more we fear a person, the more the range of responses is limited to appeasing, avoiding, or attacking him—verbally more often than physically in our culture. It is a situation frequently observed.

Love is just the opposite. Love stimulates creative imagination. "What can I do that is constructive? How can I help this person most? What can I do that will give him a new confidence in himself? How can we give her more security so that she will be more imaginative and creative, rather than rigid and domineering in her relationship with others?" The greater our love, the more we really care about the person as a person, the more resourceful and spontaneous will be our adjustment to the situation.

Determining, ourselves, to be more courageous and understanding of people, with all their individual differences; attempting to really care about all people as human beings with unfulfilled needs for love and understanding and more in need of understanding and guidance than condemnation, will help us to give our children those friendly and courageous feelings that will make it easier for them to relate to others.

CHAPTER 5

Changing Bodies Bring Changing Feelings

"I wouldn't worry," said the experienced mother of three. "When Marsha was in sixth grade I couldn't get her out of jeans, but when she hit the seventh I couldn't get her to wear them even on the coldest and stormiest days. Something just gets into them and they want to look like ladies, I guess."

This warm and understanding mother, who had never taken a course on the psychology of adolescence had learned by experience what mothers now can learn by reading—that changing bodies bring changing feelings.

Confusion from Earlier Maturing

There is a tremendous variation in growth patterns. Some children develop early, some late, but the largest number follow a sort of midway pattern. Girls mature sexually almost two years earlier than boys and follow a quite different pattern of growth. This earlier development on the part of the girls brings marked changes in the growing relationship between the sexes which has been confusing to both youngsters and parents.

"I'm not particularly concerned about the girls' being so boy crazy now," said the mother of a fifth-grade girl, "because I know that in a year or two the boys will be too interested in sports to pay much attention to them." Here again, an experienced mother with two older children had observed a significant fact that was helping her with the third: that the steadily growing interest in the other sex which takes place during the early school years gets a setback during the junior-high school period. Interest of boys in sports may be part of the reason, but probably much more basic is the fact that beginning about the seventh grade the girls forge ahead more rapidly in their growth.

After a year of slow growth, preadolescent girls suddenly begin to develop rapidly, and for a period of almost exactly two years, they grow twice as fast as at any other period in their life. By the end of the eighth grade, the girls on the average not only are taller and heavier than boys, but have developed so that they look much more mature than the boys.

This is all very confusing to both sexes. They have grown up in a world in which, by and large, men are bigger and stronger, and girls are smaller and prettier. But at this stage, the sex roles are just reversed—the girls are bigger and stronger, and the boys are smaller and prettier—or so both sexes feel.

This tendency of the girls to outgrow the boys during the seventh and eighth grades causes the boys unconsciously to resent girls. Because the boys are made to feel inferior, they compensate by acting just the opposite. "Girls are the bunk; all they do is primp and try to make themselves look pretty," they are apt to say. They tend to feel uncomfortable around the more mature girls, so they retreat into the stag line where they have the moral support of other boys. It takes good adult leadership or feminine initiative, as evidenced in girls' tag dances, to involve a great many of them in social dancing. Square dances are easier for boys at this stage, since it is simpler to fill in a square than ask a girl to dance, and the dancing itself is not so intimately face to face.

Girls continue their growing interest in the boys until they begin to resent the boys' reactions toward them. As the boys "act big" because they feel small, tease the girls because they feel uncomfortable with them, the natural tendency is for the girls to look toward older boys who have finished their growth spurt and who are now getting interested in girls again. The boys prefer to be with boys for a few years; and then, when they start dating, they look toward younger girls with whom they feel more nearly equal and therefore more comfortable. This accounts in part for the tendency during the late adolescent period for girls to continue to date older fellows. Another factor is that girls are ready to marry younger than boys because of the economic situation, although the increasing tendency of women to continue working after marriage may equalize this reason somewhat.

School leaders, in attempting to improve the relations between the sexes during this period, have tried and suggested a number of adjustments. The junior high school seems to be an improvement on the older European eight-four grade division.

Some educators have suggested that since girls are apparently about a half year more mature than boys at age six, we should consider starting girls to kindergarten and first grade six months earlier, thus reducing somewhat the adolescent problem. The most immediately practical approach, however, seems to be that of teaching seventh and eighth graders about adolescent development, particularly their temporary reversal of sex roles because of the earlier development of the girls. Where this approach has been tried, it seems to have reduced the boys' unconscious resentment toward the girls, rendered both boys and girls more comfortable with each other during this period, and made both more sympathetic for the early-developing girl and the late-developing boy.

One Girls League was unanimous in feeling that the assembly program in which problems of adolescence had been frankly discussed had been the most valuable of the year because "the boys have shown us more consideration and friendliness since then."

During these years boys and girls are struggling to become men and women. The terms "self-conscious" and "sex-conscious" have often been used to characterize this period. They are both accurate. We are all self-conscious but are just not aware of it when all goes well and we feel comfortable about ourselves. All these marked changes in their bodies make youngsters of this age very much aware of themselves and very much aware of their developing sexual natures. One of the crucial developmental tasks of children of this age is to mature normally into men and women, and again become comfortable with their own bodies and with those of the other sex.

Any deviation from normal growth intensifies their *self-* and *sex*-consciousness and explains much of the tension of this period. Normal development is so varied that each adolescent seems to *feel* a little off the beam and keeps trying to get back to a comfortable average, when in reality there is none.

Because of the fact that first menstruation is preceded by and associated with the development of the breasts and the broadening of the hips, which can be noticed by others, both sexes are conscious of the marked difference in the *time* of sexual development, which takes place largely in a two-year period. Being different may make one proud or hostile, depending upon the differences.

Take, for example, two girl cousins who had been very close friends. The families had always spent their summers together at a mountain cabin, and they lived close enough to each other for the girls to get together almost at will. Despite a year of difference in their ages they got along wonderfully, the younger accepting and enjoying the older cousin's leadership. But when Jane, the older, entered high school the relationship changed completely. The high school girl wanted nothing to do with her cousin Esther. Jane's mother, who wanted the relationship to remain cordial, tried to arrange a few activities that would throw the girls together naturally and restore the friendship, since the eighth grader's feelings were being hurt by her cousin's coldness.

Then, one evening at one of the high school PTA meetings for the parents of freshmen, a psychologist spoke on adolescent development and some of the problems of relationship created when certain girls outgrew their friends or fell behind the group. It suddenly dawned on Jane's mother that this was the problem. Her ninth-grade daughter was falling behind while the little cousin Esther had suddenly shot up and was now taller and more mature than her older cousin. "Jane is simply green with jealousy," the mother told the psychologist after the talk, and got some suggestions from him for ways of approaching the problem with her daughter. Fortunately, Jane's family had been lining up and marking their daughter's growth on the inside of a closet door every three months, and it was easy to point out that she was rapidly catching up with her younger cousin and on the way to becoming a very attractive young lady. The book *Teen Days* also helped to bolster her sagging self-esteem, and she was able to accept Esther on more friendly terms again. The relationship between them, however, was never so close as before. It probably would not have been anyway, since both girls were becoming more interested in boys than in each other.

Need for Special Help

The transition from childhood to adulthood is very difficult for both the early developing girl and the late developing boy. It is easy to see why this fact would be true. Girls forge ahead of boys during this period, but the girl who forges ahead of the other girls is completely isolated from the boys in her class.

She, more than the other girls, is apt to receive the brunt of the boys' hostility. As one girl asked her counselor, "Why are the boys so mean to me this year? I've always gotten along with them before. But this year they are just plain nasty. Just this afternoon one of them said, 'Hi, pug ugly,' when he passed me in the corridor. I'm not ugly, am I?" she pleaded with the counselor for reassurance.

"Of course, you are not ugly," he assured her. "But I think I know why a boy might say a thing like that. I'll bet it was one of the smaller fellows, wasn't it?"

"Yes, it was. As a matter of fact, he's about the smallest kid in the class, I guess. But how did you know?"

He was then able to explain to her how her early maturing was resented by the boys because it had made them feel inferior and inadequate. He went on with a well-directed question to give her a chance to talk out her own feelings: "I don't suppose you feel very comfortable either about being the biggest person in the class, do you? Just how does it feel?"

"I feel awful—like an overgrown elephant," she commented ruefully. "Will I ever stop growing?"

"When did you have your first menstrual period?" he asked her.

"Just about two months ago," she informed him.

"Then you may relax," he reassured her, "for with first menstruation, the period of rapid growth normally comes to a stop. Whatever the glandular changes are that bring about menstruation, they apparently also bring on the capping of the long bones of the arms and legs. You are just about as tall right now as you will ever be. From now on, other girls will be catching up with you, and in another year or two, most of the boys will pass you."

"Will I always be a tall girl?"

"How did you compare with the other girls up to about the fifth grade?" he asked her.

"I've always been one of the tallest girls in the class, but not the way I am now. I just outgrew all my clothes—and I guess all my friends—last year. The only ones that are nice to me are the ninth-grade boys."

Such are the problems of the early-developing girl. Not only the boys in her class resent her, but the girls too are often jealous of her more feminine look. "Let's not ask her," one seventh-grade girl was heard to remark of another. "She's so boy crazy it's funny."

Resented by the boys, shut out by the increasingly "cliquey" girls, it is easy for her to become an isolate—more comfortable alone than with others her age. "I just can't understand my daughter," one mother commented. "She has always been a leader in her church group. But this year she doesn't even want to go to the church group half the time. She just seems to want to sit home with a book. Should I force her to go?"

Definitely not. The mother should encourage her to go in a pleasant sort of way, but will be wise not to force her; she will ask questions of the girl with an "I'm puzzled" feeling rather than an "I have a right to know" attitude. If the girl opens up and talks about what's bothering her, the mother is an interested, but not an overly concerned listener. If she just clams up, the mother respects her reserve and continues to love her. Home is one place where the girl should feel completely accepted. Above all, her parents must be sympathetic toward any evidences of physical or social awkwardness, rather than irritated by them. Some casual positive suggestions, such as "You've probably just been growing so fast you haven't had time to get used to your new body yet; you'll feel more comfortable with yourself in a few months," may take root, and the girl may develop more positive attitudes. Criticizing her for not being more social will only make her more self-conscious. She must not be expected to be reasonable about it —this is a matter of *feeling*, and it probably confuses her as much as it does her parents. Youngsters need affection most when they are most unlovable. And at times, they just want to be left alone. They should have an opportunity for privacy, and it should be respected. Being patient, and encouraging the feeble efforts to be sociable they occasionally make is the best parents can do to help them through this stage. If in doubt as to how serious the problem is, it would be well for the parent to talk to the school counselor or the school psychologist, or the minister, but not to try to get the girl to do so. Learning how the girl can best be helped is a first step for the parent. If the psychologist feels he needs to talk with the girl, he will suggest it and probably get in touch with her himself.

This is an excellent time for the young girl to learn or improve some skill. If her piano has been neglected for a year or two, the mother might inquire whether she would like to start taking lessons again; or she can merely express appreciation when the girl sits down and plays. With all the clothes she needs with which to replace those she has outgrown, sewing might be an excellent and constructive pastime. More than the customary number of family picnics, outings, and other activities can be planned if she seems to enjoy them, and the girl can be encouraged to invite some friend to go along if she seems interested, even though it may inconvenience the family. The wise parent, however, does not try to force or select friendships for her.

The *late-developing boy* also needs special help. First the girls outgrow him, and then the boys. He is the runt of the group—at least he is very apt to feel that way unless he has been a successful boy during the preceding years. If he is the eager and aggressive type, he will probably compensate for his smallness by acting big. Parents can be thankful if he does, for that is much better for him than giving up and withdrawing. Lacking adult understanding and help, he may curry favor with the bigger boys in the class by needling the teacher, particularly if it is a woman the boys dislike. He may try to get attention and approval by being funny and making the group laugh. (Some of our comedians were probably late-developing boys who made the situation pay off.) Or he may become a "tough guy" trying to prove that even though he is small he is no sissy. He may prove how big he is by bullying younger children or by smoking cigarettes; or how brave he is by stealing from the corner drugstore or driving the family car when his parents are away. The next step may be to "borrow" someone else's car. Car thefts are often traced to little boys who act big.

Most late-developing boys can be spared serious adjustment problems if parents encourage them to develop skill in some sport where size is not an important factor. In ping-pong and diving, for example, co-ordination is much more important than size. Investment in a ping-pong table, a set of golf clubs and some lessons, or a tennis racquet would be a small price to pay to help a late-developing fourteen- or fifteen-year-old, if he is athletically inclined. A musical instrument and a chance to play in the school band or orchestra can do wonders for a boy's morale. Dramatics, choir, and other group experiences are also constructive. If ever a boy needs a dad, this is the boy. Taking time to play ball with him or go fishing with him, or developing a mutual interest in sports, might make the difference between a normal and a delinquent youngster, providing, of course, that the relationship is a mutually enjoyable and satisfying one.

The problems of the early-developing girl and the late-developing boy are so important that a discussion of them at the onset of adolescence should be included in the school curriculum for every youngster. It should help these young people feel better about themselves, and improve the other teen-agers' attitude toward them. It is particularly helpful for the late-developing boy to know that he will be taller, in comparison with his birth height, than he would have been if he had developed when the others did, since he probably comes from short stock to begin with. It is quite reassuring for him to know that once he starts, he will grow about eight inches, on the average, in the next couple of years.

The endocrinologist—a doctor who specializes in studying glands and their mysterious secretions—is learning how to start that adolescent growth spurt in the boy who has not begun it by the time he is a senior in high school. This specialist can at times also be very helpful in slowing or stopping rapid growth in the unusually tall girl. Realizing the problems that exceptionally early or late development can cause, it is hoped parents may be more inclined to seek the medical or psychological assistance which may be so helpful to many.

Early Crushes—a Phase of Love-Sex Feelings

The maturing pituitary gland, which apparently causes the bodily changes associated with puberty, probably also affects the other ductless glands, since they are all interrelated. In any case, there seem to be stirrings of new feelings, partly sexual and partly emotional, which represent more mature love-sex feelings than the young boy or girl has experienced before. A strong attraction may develop for a member of the other sex who is older—a teacher, an athlete, a movie star, an attractive neighbor. Such a person may be married or single; it does not matter since this is "one way" loving. No response is needed from the object of affection. It is enough to love and adore.

For the girl, the mere thought of her "lover" brings a surge of good feeling. In her dreams he returns her love and affection, making her feel wonderful. If her hero should smile at her, it would be almost more than she could bear. But any real approach from him would probably frighten her since she is not ready to meet the demands a real relationship would make upon her. She is "in love with love," and he happens at the moment to be the object of her love. All she asks is to be allowed to dream in peace. Her apparent resentment at being asked to set the table for dinner may be due largely to the fact that she has been brought back to earth with a thud.

The boy, too, tends often to idolize some more mature girl or woman. It may be his teacher, a movie actress, the chum of an older sister—almost any attractive feminine creature will do. He worships her from afar. In one essential, however, his dream differs from that of the girl described above: his dreams may be sexually colored. He may not be content merely to think of her as his sweetheart; he may think of her as his wife. This permits him to have imaginary sexual intercourse with her. These dreams may trigger his earliest attempts at masturbation. He may carry on this imaginary marriage for months on end, and experience, in embryo, some of the love-sex feelings he projects forward into his own marriage at some later date.

These early "crushes" are of more than passing interest because they portray a phase of the development of love-sex feelings. They also seem to foreshadow some sex differences that continue into more mature patterns of response. Whether the greater tendency of the boy to have sexually colored daydreams is due to sexual tensions originating in a developing physiological urge; whether he is more sensitive to visual and imaginative sexual stimulation than girls; or whether it is something he has picked up from his boy culture or from exposure to older boys or men, is difficult to say.

Suffice it here to point out that the fantasies accompanying these early crushes are different for boys and for girls. The girl dreams of yielding to the embraces of her phantom lover with generalized good feeling, but does not fantasy genital involvement. The boy, on the other hand, may have the same romantic feelings about the girl of his dreams, but in his fantasy he may win also her feminine surrender to his sexual ardor. But two needs they have in common: each is satisfying a *need to love* a member of the other sex, and each is imaginatively winning a sought *response* from the loved partner. Out of such initial successes may grow the courage to reach out in love at some later date to a *real* sweetheart and anticipate a favorable response. The seeds of heterosexual love, planted by the love expressed by father and mother for each other and for the child, produce their first delicate buds in the crushes of early adolescence. Parents must appreciate their tender beauty and nourish them with interest and understanding—not with the teasing and ridicule of a past generation.

Homosexual Tendencies—Unsatisfied Needs?

This imaginary romance stage seems to lead naturally into the first timid attempts at reaching out for love by growing boys and girls. The imaginary romance stage required no response, or even awareness, on the part of the object of love; but this new stage is characterized by little "probing actions" to test out ability to win a love response from another person. Typically, these are safest and easiest with a member of their own sex. Hence this is sometimes referred to as the homosexual, or gang, stage of development. The "homo" in homosexual comes from the Greek, meaning *same* (not from the Latin "homo" meaning *man*). It is the opposite of *hetero*sexual, meaning *different*. When applied to this stage it means simply that both boys and girls, for a period of time, seem to be more comfortable with members of their own sex than with the other sex. This discussion, however, is not concerned with the "gang" or social aspects so much as with the interpersonal relationships involving love-sex feelings.

The only characteristic which this phase of development has in common with adult homosexuality, is that it is probably a setback or flight reaction from a continually more intimate relationship with the other sex. Girls almost universally hit this stage first. Their feelings of rejection by boys of their own age, occasioned by the girls' earlier development, probably draw them more closely together as girls for a sense of security and belonging. During the seventh and eighth grades it is quite common, for example, to see girls walking along together with their arms around each other. They frequently dance together and show definite tendencies to pair off and have bosom pals. They spend every available moment with each other and, five minutes after they are separated, they are on the telephone talking together in conversations that go on and on, much to the irritation of the family. If this were a boy and girl relationship, this great attentiveness to each other would certainly be interpreted as "going steady" or a love relationship. Earlier dating may be shortening this phase of development in our culture.

Certainly there is no cause for concern regarding it. There would be more basis for concern if our daughter did not have some bosom-pal relationship or, on the other hand, if she failed to move on from this phase into dating and normal heterosexual relationships during adolescence. For example, a housemother consulted a college dean regarding her concern about two girls living in the dormitory who she felt were continuing this normal seventh- and eighth-grade girl pattern on into their freshman year at college.

These girls had remained close friends through high school. Both girls had dated only a few times, and they had chosen to go to the same college and to be roommates. The dean of women asked the school psychologist to discuss the situation with them. After a series of conferences with each of the roommates separately, the girls began to see the nature of their problem. At the end of the semester they accepted the wisdom of having new roommates. Once aware of the problem, both girls seemed willing and anxious to improve their heterosexual adjustment.

To the average American, the term *homosexual* instantly calls to mind a perverted sexual relationship between two adults for purely physical satisfactions. This probably accounts for the shocked response to Kinsey's book on the male, which reported such a high incidence of homosexuality. The confusion arises over the term. Though many Americans divide people into only two classes—normally heterosexual or pervertedly homosexual—Dr. Kinsey uses the term more broadly, classifying as homosexual any sexual stimulation by a member of one's own sex, either psychological or physical. For example, he included sex play between young boys as a homosexual outlet in reporting male sex activities. In his later work on the female, he clarifies his use of the term further by dividing women into seven categories, ranging from the totally homosexual, to the totally heterosexual, with one classification, containing some 15 per cent of the women studied, of those who had never experienced either psychologic or physically erotic sexual feelings toward either a man or a woman.

Most people are bisexual in the sense of having warm, affectionate feelings for members of both sexes. Some persons consider being a "man hater" or a "woman hater" with regard to the other sex almost as abnormal as feeling attraction only for a member of one's own sex. Because of the more generalized nature of their sexual response, probably girls and women experience more sexual feelings in their intimate relationships than they are aware of —for example, girls who enjoy dancing with either boys or girls.

With boys, because sexual arousal is more localized in the genitals, they are more aware of it. Often a wrestling type of horseplay sets off parallel or mutual sex play. Dr. Kinsey states (Volume I, page 167): "It is not improbable that nearly all boys have some preadolescent genital play with other boys or with girls. Only about one-fifth as many of the girls have such play." His statement is based on his findings that 70 per cent of the preadolescent boys themselves report such play, whereas only half remember it by the time they are adult. He assumes that many of the 30 per cent who did not report it, had forgotten. When one realizes that he considers any erotic feelings for a member of one's own sex, even though there is no physical contact, as homosexual, his statistics seem more valid and less alarming.

Boys may have homosexual experiences with other boys, or with adult males, for a variety of reasons: curiosity, as a group experience in which one has to participate to maintain status, as a sex thrill, because of the persuasiveness of an older male, and so on. But for the vast majority of the youngsters who have these experiences they are just that—experiences. Our chief concern should be to understand what the behavior means to the person involved, and try to help him find more acceptable ways of satisfying his basic needs.

Many were alarmed by the disclosure of the first Kinsey report that there were apparently both more premarital intercourse and more homosexual activity than they had suspected. But Dr. O. Spurgeon English, Professor of Psychiatry at Temple University Medical School, was not dismayed. Writing in *Parents Magazine* in October, 1948, he said: "Rightly interpreted and understood, the Kinsey report should greatly hearten and encourage every thoughtful mother and father, for it indicates the deep instinctual drive of every human being for close touch with others. It shows that no man wants to live unto himself alone. . . . If it shows too, that some of the methods used in the search for union are mistaken ones, that is our chance to correct the mistakes and improve the methods."

Children will always want, and need, intimate human relationships. If they learn from parents how to win love from others, they will never be satisfied, at least for long, with any kind of sexual relationship in which love is not the dominant factor.

Stronger Attractions

Gradually the boys, at first in company with other boys, begin to "hang around" where the girls are apt to be. They still may lack the confidence to approach them directly, but they make it easy for the girls to approach them, and the girls usually find some excuse to do so. At first they are open about it. A "girls tag" dance is usually very successful, whereas a "boys tag" is apt to fall flat on its face. Gradually the girls learn to be more indirect, using flirtation to attract boys, encouraging them to talk with them or ask them to dance. Still later a girl learns to be more subtle, limiting her "aggressiveness" to smiling at the boy, looking in his direction, and showing obvious interest. It is often the girl who first *feels* a real interest in a particular boy, and in many ways, perhaps even unconsciously, lets him know of that interest. The girl or woman who waits for a male to "come a-courtin'" may keep right on waiting.

And so, very early, the boys begin to respond to the

girls' interest in them. Apparently ignoring the girls entirely, the boys "put on a great act" of manly activities, horseplay, boastful talk or stunts, or secretive whispering, glancing from time to time to make sure the girls are watching. They are stimulated by girls, and they like to be near them, but they are not ready to take much initiative in the relationship.

Preadolescent boys are often pressured into social dancing by girls and adults before they are ready for that degree of intimacy with the other sex. Some adults are beginning to feel that this tendency to rush both boys and girls into the dancing and pairing-off relationships formerly associated with the high school and college groups may cause more emotional insecurity than satisfaction. There is even some evidence to indicate that youngsters who start going steady very early have more emotional problems than those who first experience these relationships during the late high school and college years. The most comprehensive study of engagements indicates that later adjustment seems to be associated with early teen-age "parties" more than with early dating experiences. Opportunity to experience companionship with the other sex, without the consideration for the other person demanded by "pairing off" relationships—for example, mixer games and folk dancing rather than social dancing—would seem best geared to the needs of the preadolescent.

This is the "try out" period. Children are trying out other youngsters, both boys and girls, for companionship. But probably most of all they are trying out their own abilities and skills in human relations. Almost all of them will need encouragement at times. For the first time in their lives they are beginning to judge themselves by adult standards and they feel quite inadequate. They are inadequate, but not for long. They tend to make excuses by saying, "I'm different." They are different, but they can be encouraged to think of difference as inevitable and good. "Sure, you're different—thank goodness! Wouldn't it be terrible if we were all alike? They feel the same way you do; they just don't show it. You don't show it either. Remember, time is in your favor." What they need most is the reassurance that they are becoming more mature, attractive, and lovable people. We must not expect them to act like adults. All we have any right to expect is growth in the right direction. If we can appreciate that fact and the effort it costs them to "grow" emotionally, if we love them and enjoy them at each stage of their development, we shall make it possible for them to feel comfortable about themselves, and others, including the other sex.

CHAPTER 6

Menstruation, Masturbation, and Other Adolescent Concerns

As children approach adolescence, some of them who have been easy to talk to before seem a bit bored when parents try to discuss problems they think the youngsters should know about. This does not mean that parents should give up, but it does mean that they should respect the reticence of youth and not plow full steam ahead, nor feel rejected if, in the growing need for independence, their boys and girls talk more freely with someone who is not so close to them. The YMCA, YWCA, Scouts, and church groups have made a valuable contribution to many young people in making available group discussions of these personal problems in an impersonal way.

Talking Together Pays Off

One father who had a national reputation in the field of sex education volunteered to talk to a Boy Scout troop and asked his son to go with him to operate the slide projector. It was the only way he could think of to break the layer of ice that seemed to have developed. It worked. On the way home, the twelve-year-old opened up with a number of good questions. In another case, a physical education instructor who could ably discuss masturbation in his classes, admitted that it wasn't easy to discuss the problem with his own son; that he had to try more than once to make an opportunity for conversation.

Many fathers do nothing, or just leave a book like Roy Dickerson's *Into Manhood* lying around in the hope that their son will find it and read it. Others are more direct, presenting the book to the boy with some such confidential statement as this: "Son, you are moving into adolescence soon, and you will be developing very rapidly, particularly sexually. This little book answers a lot of the questions that may come to your mind during the next few years. I'll be glad to discuss any of the problems with you further, if you wish." A short time later he may follow up by asking casually, as he rubs his son's back at bedtime (most boys continue to like that as long as they can

[101]

Carl A. Rudisill Library
LENOIR RHYNE COLLEGE

get it), "How did you like the book?" Sometimes the boys have read it, sometimes not.

One father's son had not. "I wish you'd read that section on 'seminal emissions' because you are approaching an age when you might experience one and I'd like you to be prepared for it," the father said. He might have dropped it there, but he went on to discuss it with the boy, explaining the release of seminal fluids during a sexually colored dream. He explained that it was not harmful in any way, but quite natural, and that it might happen any time. That was all.

About a month later his son spoke to him one evening. "Dad, you know that 'wet dream' business you told me about? Well, I've never had one. Do you think I'm normal?" he asked. Fortunately, the father had read the book before he gave it to the boy, so he said reassuringly, "Sure, you're barely fifteen. I wouldn't worry about it for at least another year. Then if you haven't had one we'll check with the doctor." A month or two later, as he was shaving one morning, his son entered the bathroom and commented casually, "Dad, I had a seminal emission last night." "Good," said his father, "I guess I'll have to start treating you like a man now, won't I?" That was all either needed to say. But it showed that the boy had read the book, and the father was able to supplement the book, particularly with reassurance.

A book is an excellent aid, if it is not used as a substitute for conversation. Talking together may be somewhat difficult for both father and son, but making the effort often pays good dividends in improved relationships and mutual understanding.

These Mistaken Ideas

Boys, of course, know about the development of the beard and look forward to growing one as proof of approaching manhood. They are not always so well informed about the range of the normal coming of pubic hair and the growth spurt with its accompanying change of voice.

Nor are they always prepared for the outbreak of pimples and blackheads that begins often about the same time the coming of "fuzz" marks the beginning of shaving. Boys seem to pass along a myth that there is some causal relation between pimples and masturbation. Cases of attempted suicide have been reported which were attributed at least in part to an unbearable sense of shame. If pimples were caused by masturbation, then they assumed their weakness and worthlessness must be obvious to everyone.

This acne, coming as it so often does during a period of bodily change and excessive self-consciousness, may cause both boys and girls to become painfully shy, particularly where parents exhibit anxiety over it. Parents and hygiene teachers can so easily point out that the condition is due to the overactivity of the oil glands in the skin. The oversecretion of oil causes irritation and the development of a "blackhead." If this is not cleansed away it may become infected, and a pimple results. Washing the face gently night and morning with toilet soap and warm water, followed by a cool rinse—and in some cases by rubbing alcohol or an after-shave lotion—normally helps. Cutting down on the intake of fats (peanut butter, chocolate, nuts) is also desirable, of course.

It goes without saying that girls need to understand the development of their breasts, but boys should understand this development, too, particularly the fact that breasts become more sensitive and can be hurt painfully in early teen-age roughhousing with boys. It is sometimes surprising what mistaken facts and distorted attitudes youngsters can get. One girl reported that she and a girl friend, noticing that their breasts were developing, decided to do something to stop it. One had heard that drinking vinegar would stunt them. She wasn't sure how much. Not having any adult to whom they felt free to go, they took enough to make them both miserably ill. Fortunately, one of their mothers found out about it and was able to help them see the development of their breasts as a natural and desirable part of becoming a woman.

In one junior high school, the principal and the

parents decided upon a joint approach. The study of human growth and reproduction was introduced into the science class, and parents were to encourage their children to relay to them what they were learning about the subject. In this way it would be easier for them to talk together, and the parents could be surer how facts and attitudes were registering. At the same time, in their naturally divided physical education classes, the boys and girls separately were given the opportunity to write out and hand in the "questions you probably didn't feel free to ask in your science class with both boys and girls present." These questions revealed that the girls wanted to know more about menstruation and feminine hygiene. The boys turned in more questions dealing with masturbation than all other topics combined.

Good Feelings About Menstruation

Menstruation does not hit like a bolt from the blue. It is preceded by the development of breasts and pubic hair. These body changes, either in one's own little girl or among the child's friends, give a natural opportunity to make sure that she is prepared for the beginning of menstruation. A girl may have known the facts for a long time, yet still be jolted when she experiences her first menstruation.

A surprising number of girls even today are not

adequately prepared. Some are confused and embarrassed. For others it is a frightening experience. One girl suffered terribly. Her only sex education had been statements such as "Never let a boy kiss you. One thing leads to another. You wouldn't want to have a baby before you are married, would you?" It so happened that a week before her first menstruation, she had attended an eighth-grade party where they had played that fascinating game enjoyed by most of us in our youth, "Spin the Bottle." During the game she had been on the receiving end of a kiss from a boy, a somewhat pleasant but disturbing experience. When her first menstruation came she was terribly upset. Lacking a true knowledge of the essential facts, she jumped to the conclusion that she was pregnant. Recalling all the remarks she had heard about unmarried mothers, she was determined not to be one. She considered running away or seeking an abortionist (she had heard of them although she was only thirteen). She even considered committing suicide. Her mother finally sensed her great distress and won her confidence enough to have her blurt out, "I'm going to have a baby."

Now it was the mother's time to be upset. Instead of doing a little questioning, she got the girl into the car and rushed her off to the doctor. An examination by the doctor and a few questions by him clarified the situation. He gave the mother a short lecture which probably only made her feel more guilty and inadequate. After all, the mother had done the best she could. She needed help, mostly in correcting her own attitudes, and some suggestions as to where she and her daughter could have obtained the correct information. A book like *Facts of Life and Love for Teen-Agers*, by Evelyn Millis Duvall, would have given daughter and mother much to talk about and provided both with much needed information.

Menstruation means "monthly flow" and can best be understood as one part of a cycle, called the menstrual cycle. It begins with ovulation, the passing of the ovum or egg from the ovary about fourteen days before the beginning of the menstrual flow of blood. At this time, a gland starts to produce a secretion which causes the lining of the uterus to begin to fill up with blood with which to nourish the fertilized egg when it enters the uterus. If the egg is fertilized, it begins to grow rapidly, dividing again and again. It develops a sticky exterior so that when it enters the uterus it can attach itself to the blood-filled lining and begin to grow there. It probably takes about a week for the egg to move through the Fallopian tubes from the ovary to the uterus.

If the egg is not fertilized, it disintegrates within a few days. In this case, the pituitary gland begins to produce another secretion which builds up and causes the uterus to shed its lining, a little blood leav-

ing the body with it. This process is called menstruation and normally lasts from three to six days. Every
woman has her own cycle which is "regularly irregular." Some women have a five- or six-day flow every
twenty-seven to thirty-one days; others are normal
having a three-day flow every twenty-six to twenty-
seven days; others are normal on a six- to eight-week
cycle. Each girl should be encouraged to start chart-
ing her menstrual flow and discover and adjust to
her own particular cycle. During the first year she
will normally be quite irregular. Even after that the
cycle will be thrown off schedule by colds, illness,
emotional upsets.

Of course, one need not go into all these details,
especially at first. Knowing that the uterus prepares
each month for the coming of a fertilized egg or eggs
and then casts off the lining when none arrives, is the
important concept together with the assurance that
the accompanying loss of blood is perfectly normal
and in no way harmful.

Regarding what can and cannot be done during
menstruation, each girl must learn for herself. In
general it is wise to avoid all extremes during this
period—extreme exercise or its opposite, extreme
temperatures, extreme diets. Going ahead as usual
seems to be a good attitude. One college girl who
had regularly stayed in bed for several days each time
she had especially heavy menstrual flow, found that

she actually felt much better when she attended classes as usual. Apparently she had acquired the idea long ago that when she had a heavy flow she was going to "feel just terrible," and so she did. But whenever she went resolutely on about her usual college program, she experienced almost no unpleasant effects.

Another college girl reported that cramps which had defied medical treatment were greatly improved after counseling, during which she gained considerable insight into her attitudes. She came to realize for the first time that her father had tried everything possible to "raise her as a boy." Most of the time she ignored the fact that she was a woman, but once a month she was reminded of her sex in no uncertain terms. Fathers and mothers who give girls boy's names, encourage them in masculine haircuts, dress, and activities, may overdo it, as apparently this father did. Mothers who succeed, by example, in making their daughters glad they are women are giving them something very important in many ways.

Bathing as usual, of course, and even more frequently so as to avoid any possibility of body odor, is important. There is much more that could be said, but probably any girl's gym teacher has some of the latest free booklets put out by the companies that produce pads and tampons.

But even more important than the purely physical

aspects, is a sense of participation on the part of the girl in the continuity of life from generation to generation. Certainly there are unpleasant aspects, but there are also the satisfactions of maturity and womanhood. One mother prepared her daughter well in advance for what to expect and why. In addition she purchased a belt and a box of pads and explained just what to do when the first flow began at home or at school. One morning her daughter marched into the kitchen with her head high and a new look in her eye. "You're going to treat me like a lady from now on, Mother," she announced proudly, "I've grown up." How different from the frightened girl described earlier! This girl felt pride in herself and in her sexual maturity. She accepted herself and her sex.

A Better Understanding of Masturbation

Nearly a century ago, a doctor, too embarrassed to sign his name, wrote a book called *Satan and Society* in which he described in great detail the terrible consequences of masturbation—"self-abuse" as he called it. Today, a physician reading the book would assure us that the famous cases reported were not young people suffering from masturbation but from tuberculosis, defective vision, stomach ulcers, acne, and a host of now commonly diagnosed disorders. The good physician apparently "got hepped" on masturbation and found on questioning that each of his victims had been guilty. Had the doctor made a simple, general check, instead of writing a book, he would have discovered that most of the healthy young people around him were equally "guilty."

The more science has learned about our sexual natures and functioning, the more reassuring it has been that masturbation is a normal experience of growing up. It does not cause mental retardation and it is a factor in mental illness only where excessive anxiety or guilt feelings have resulted in self-destructive tendencies. The "manly fluids" are recognized to be internal secretions called hormones which are absorbed directly into the blood stream and are not expelled from the body in the semen. Further, we know that there is no danger of "depleting" the reproductive sperm. Nature produces billions of sperms for every one that fertilizes an ovum, and man's fertility continues practically all his life.

Masturbation is an almost universal experience for adolescent boys. The frequency varies tremendously from boy to boy, the highest incidence occurring in early adolescence. In an early study of the practice among college men, 96 per cent reported having masturbated to some degree.

Why should there be so much concern about a practice which has been so universally experienced? Masturbation has been practiced by boys who later became good husbands and good fathers as well as by those who did not, and it apparently occurs at one time or another during the growing-up process of many boys and girls. Is it not the power of the sex drive that is feared? Does not preoccupation with this drive, or the exploitation of others to satisfy it, create much misery and unhappiness? Does not the use of sex for purely sensual satisfaction strengthen the physical appetites? What about our mental, aesthetic, and spiritual needs?

What is the real question here? How can one's highest values best be preserved? Is not the power of sex a potential value as well as a threat? Is fear the best focus, the best instrument of control?

Psychiatrists, from Freud to the present day, have been concerned about anything which causes men to reject physical desires as bad in themselves, because of the unwholesome guilt feelings so often produced. A boy who has been led to believe that masturbation is a sin against God and an indication of lack of character and self-control, *may* refrain from masturbation, but he probably will not. He is then likely to feel guilty and "no good." Such an attitude may produce anxiety and increased tension, and may lead to further masturbation with increased guilt feelings.

But let us suppose that the fear of committing a sin is sufficient to prevent masturbation. Does that solve his problem? Not according to Dr. Karl Menninger

(*Pastoral Psychology,* December, 1954, page 29): "All psychiatric experience confirms the view that the boy who refrains from masturbation out of fear and guilt is more unstable, more subject to physical and nervous breakdowns, more likely to develop character disturbances than the boy who is able to masturbate without guilt, or to control such guilt feelings as masturbation arouses in him."

Sometimes a child may feel guilty about masturbation even when parents do their best not to give him any reason to feel so. He may sense the power of the sex drive, and fear lest it gain too much control. How can we help? By adding to his fear and shame or by strengthening his faith? As preparation for a positive approach, let us look at some of the factors that bear on this problem of masturbation.

Apparently both boys and girls are stimulated by such physical contact as dancing, necking, and petting. But in addition, boys are stimulated just as strongly, and far more frequently, by seeing or just imagining sexually stimulating objects or situations. In view of the barrage of sexually exciting stimuli that boys experience in motion pictures, television, advertising, at the swimming pool or at the beach, and at school, it is almost surprising that incidence and frequency of masturbation is not much higher than it was a generation ago.

For a young boy, a stimulus does not have to be

sexual to be sexually exciting. About forty nonsexual types of excitement have been found to lead to erection among preadolescent and early teen-age boys. The list includes such things as fast bicycle riding, being scared, being alone at night, being yelled at, war motion pictures, anger. Even a full bladder may stimulate sexual arousal, and many boys awaken nearly every morning with an erect penis. A college girl, reviewing some material on the male sex drive, wrote: "I have always felt sorry for women because of their monthly period. But I guess we have no real sex problem when compared with the persistent and insistent sex urges of a boy or young man."

Masturbation does not seem to be so widespread a problem for girls as for boys, although girls may suffer just as much if not more from guilt feelings. Probably because many girls get little sexual stimulation from visual or imaginative stimuli, they do not talk much about sex, exchange "sexy" pictures or stories, or do to any extent the many other things boys do for a "sexual kick." Whereas some masturbation is almost universal among boys, only about half of the women studied by Kinsey report such experiences, and half of those discovered the practice by themselves, whereas three-fourths of the boys were "exposed" to it much earlier by older boys. The girls who reported masturbation did not begin so early nor masturbate so frequently, and whereas three-fourths of the boys accompanied masturbation with sexual fantasy, only about half of the girls and women did so.

It is important for girls to understand the repetitive nature of stimulation to orgasm. Until a girl has experienced orgasm, she apparently experiences no *urge* to do so. With each experience, however, the desire to repeat the experience is normally increased. Since, in our culture, many boys depend largely on girls to set the limits to their intimacy, there is a real question whether the girl who has frequently experienced orgasm through masturbation may not become more easily and completely aroused by the normal intimacies of dancing, necking, and petting, than the girl who has seldom or never experienced intense sexual arousal.

Fear that youngsters are "going to the dogs" does not seem justified. Comparison of the older with the younger generation shows an amazing similarity of patterns. The data indicate that the old fear campaign was not successful in preventing masturbation, nor has the absence of any concerted effort to prevent it during recent years greatly increased it. Although there has been a slight increase in the percentage masturbating, particularly among the college group, only about half as many have had contacts with prostitutes.

It seems clear that masturbation is not likely to

become a permanent substitute satisfaction for sexual intercourse. The latter seems to have almost universal preference—and rightly so. Masturbation is a solitary and predominantly physical satisfaction; heterosexual intercourse between people in love is not only a physical pleasure but satisfies an even deeper need to give and receive love. Only one who fails in his love relationships would be content with the limited physical and social satisfactions of masturbation.

We apparently need have no fear that adolescent boys who think of girls sexually and are stimulated by them will become aggressive sexually as a result of their masturbation. Research might indicate just the opposite. Dr. Noel Keys and others have reported their impressions from casual talks with boys of certain economic and religious groups: namely, that those who showed greatest embarrassment when they were questioned about masturbation, and denied masturbating, were often the most open in bragging about their sexual exploits. In their gang standards or "peer culture" there was nothing wrong with "making" a girl. Only those who could not win a sex partner resorted to masturbation, hence were looked upon as masculine failures. The college group apparently has very different attitudes toward both intercourse and masturbation, masturbating about twice as often as the least educated group, but having premarital intercourse only about one-tenth as often. College students seem to marry later, but also more permanently and more happily than the others.

What can parents do about masturbation? The first thing they can do is to recognize that their own feelings about it root in their own upbringing. Attitudes toward masturbation have probably changed more in the last generation than those toward any other phase of sex activity. A real desire to accept it as a normal part of development seems an important first step.

Can parents accept the fact that body sensations are as God-given as their minds, and will they have confidence that their children can learn to use them constructively?

The random rubbing of the genitals by either little boys or girls will not, normally, be sufficiently rewarding to cause frequent repetition or the formation of a habit. With the approach of adolescence and the capacity for the ejaculation of fluids by boys it is more likely to become repetitive.

Even when masturbation becomes repetitive, modern medicine assures us, there is no danger of physical harm and no danger of excess unless the practice is complicated by externally stimulating situations or by guilt and anxiety tensions. Masturbation to excess is usually considered to be the *result* rather than the *cause* of emotional or social problems. For example, the shy youngster, cut off from normal social relations with the other sex, may compensate with imaginary sexual relations in masturbation. His masturbation results from his social isolation rather than causing it. Helping adolescents to have many friends in both sexes and encouraging them to make the adjustments which such friendships require, not only reduces the need for masturbation, but aids in a good all-round social adjustment.

Apparently anything that can be done to reduce the tension in their lives and help them to be more at peace with themselves and the world, will reduce the unconscious desire for the release of tension through masturbation. The more they can be helped to find real satisfactions in their personal activities and social relations the less they will be inclined to desire a "substitute satisfaction."

Are parents helping their children to develop self-discipline on the basis of self-understanding? "He that ruleth himself is greater than he that taketh a city." Parents who depend primarily upon obedience to external authority for control, will be defeated because masturbation by its very nature is a secret and private activity.

Do parents take the necessary time to allow their boys and girls to make their own choices and do they reward socially approved choices with a word of appreciation and approval? Are parents *also*, as a bal-

ance, encouraging them to listen to their own conscience and to do what they think is right? Youngsters
who at times fail to exercise reasonable self-control
often develop healthy guilt feelings which act as a
brake against excess.

Does a child have enough confidence in the love
and understanding of his parents to feel that he has
their emotional support, not their condemnation?

In a sexually stimulating environment like ours
with the long adolescent period, there will be times
when a boy is sexually stimulated beyond reasonable
control. Helping him to reduce the frequency of
masturbation, rather than to stop it entirely, has
proved to be a more achievable goal.

A boy or girl needs to feel that it is not abnormal
to indulge in occasional masturbation, but that it is
normal to learn to control and direct energy toward
more permanent achievements and satisfactions—
getting an education, achieving in sports, dramatics,
music or other forms of social recreation; and making the effort to develop a good relationship with
the other sex, one of whom he or she may someday
want to marry. The long dating and courtship period
requires real sexual control if one is to make choices
in terms of a happy marriage rather than immediate
physical pleasures.

Even within marriage, sex urges must be controlled in the interest of sexual harmony and mutual

desire. The important thing would seem to be that the restraint be self-imposed through choice, not through fear.

Avoiding sexually stimulating situations reduces desire. One teen-ager commented that taking down the pictures of seductive pin-up girls and substituting sports pictures had helped; another, that avoiding the fellows who were always telling "sexy" stories helped. Other boys have said that a different attitude on dates made the biggest difference. Instead of trying to see how far they could go with necking or petting, they found that if they set out to show the girl a really wonderful time, and to be themselves the kind of men they would feel proud to be, far less sexual stimulation and resultant masturbation resulted.

A number of older boys have reported that it was very helpful, when they were sexually stimulated by a girl, to think of her in terms of love rather than exploitation. For example, instead of imagining having intercourse with her, they would say to themselves, "I hope the girl I marry someday will be as sexually attractive as she is." Even if they were stimulated to the point of masturbation, imagining being married to the girl left them "with a more decent feeling" than they would have had in imagining a purely physical relationship with her.

In the end, the fantasy, which in the case of most

boys accompanies masturbation, may prove to be the significant factor. If the intensely pleasant feelings are associated with a series of exploitative physical relationships, they may develop into a kind of substitute satisfaction that makes marriage seem unnecessary or even limiting. If they are associated with love and marriage, they may well be a positive factor motivating the individual toward marriage.

Adolescence is a period of rapid development. It is also the period when the dreams of a youth become the foundations for the man he is to become. Dreams may be aspirations leading to increased drive toward the rewards envisioned; or they may be escapist, embodying the things he fears will never be his to enjoy in real life. What makes the difference? Is it the sense of personal worth? Is it the sense of security that comes when one has parents who care? Is it the history of successes and failures that span the years? Or is it all these—and more?

If children have faith in their future because their parents have helped them to make previous dreams come true, then they will be more ready to take in stride the changes that occur in adolescence. They will not fear their impulses, but will have confidence in their ability increasingly to make wiser and more satisfying choices.

CHAPTER 7

Growth of Love-Sex Feelings During Early Adolescence

Adolescence in our culture is a period of transition in many phases of personal development. But, most important, it is the period between sexual and emotional maturity—the period between the time young people become sexually capable of becoming parents, and the time they become emotionally more capable of the kind of love and kind of responsibility that is necessary to successful parenthood. Because they have as their ideal a monogamous or one-man, one-woman relationship based upon love and lasting a lifetime, our young people do not *mate* as mammals do when they become sexually mature, but wait, ideally, for more mature love, and economic and social competence, and then *marry*. They make a great deal of *marriage* because they want it to last. For most young people, it is an event which marks a distinct break with the family in which they grew up, and the beginning of the family they create for themselves.

Adolescence is also a period of transition from accepted *dependence* upon adults, through a period in which young people wrest a certain amount of *independence* from parents and other adults, and then move on, ideally, into a more mature *interdependence* that characterizes a successful marriage or, for that matter, almost any kind of adult relationship. These important psychological stages are phases both of their love-sex relations and of their work and responsibility relations. However, because this is not primarily a book on adolescence but about love-sex feelings, the discussion will be limited to that phase of development. How can adults encourage the development of increasingly mature love-sex feelings in children and discourage immature or exploitative love-sex behavior?

There is certainly no one way to do it. Each parent must build upon his own past experiences, upon his children's many experiences during the early years, and upon his relationship with them during adolescence. But increased understanding of normal love-sex development by both youngsters and their parents, coupled with "I love you and I'm trying to understand you" feelings on the part of each for the other, seems to make for the best working relations. Good relations between parents and teen-agers help the teen-ager with his relations with his peers—particularly, perhaps, with members of the other sex.

Adolescents Need Much Love

It is easy for parents to see that the small and rather helpless baby or child needs to be loved to feel secure. It is difficult for them to realize that a cocky, sarcastic, and independent adolescent needs to feel loved. But that need is exactly why he is cocky, sarcastic, and independent. Because he is not sure of himself and yet senses an increasing demand for more adult behavior, he may act very sure of himself. Because he feels suddenly rather inferior to the adults with whom he has begun to compare himself, he may try, unconsciously, through sarcasm to cut them down to his size so that he will not feel inferior. And because he is increasingly frustrated to realize that his dream of "doing just as I please" when he grows up is not going to come true, he acts more than ever independent in the ways he dares be independent. All his life, when he has felt frustrated, he has said to himself, "When I'm grown up, I'm going to. . . ." He is beginning to realize that most adults do not do as they please; they do as the situation demands; they do what earning a living, bringing up children, having friends, and being respected demands. He hates to give up his dream—as he once hated to give up the idea of Santa Claus—and he may turn this hatred on those around him against whom it is safe to strike out. He dares not strike out openly at his teachers; he dares not strike out too violently against his friends, or he will have none. The one group that will continue to tolerate him, no matter how hostile he acts, is normally his family, and so he strikes out at them. Of course, he may be punished, but he has worked off his hostility, and tomorrow he can say, "I'm sorry," two of the most magical words in the English language. All will be loving and understanding again—*if* his parents understand that when he is least lovable, he is most in need of love.

However, even if parents desire to give their adolescent boy or girl love, they are often confused by the reaction to their attempts. Adolescents no longer want to be shown affection as they have been in the past, for that makes them feel they are still being treated like a child. Parents have to discover new ways to show love and affection. For the boy, the parents may show keen interest in his hobbies or ideas of the moment, encouraging him to talk by asking how his favorite team fared the day before, when the fishing season opens, how his classes are going. A little wrestling with "the old man" may give him a chance to assert his growing strength. A pat on the back, roughing up his hair smilingly, or chatting with him just before he goes to sleep—such things make him feel respected and loved.

Fathers are important to their daughters, too, during this period. Mother was the most important person in the girl's love life for so many years that she tends to be associated with childhood. Dad has been the man of the world who goes out into the world each day. Now that she is eager to try her wings, she wants help from the man who knows how. As a twelve-year-old girl expressed it in asking a question about women, "I've talked to Mommy, but I want to know how men feel about it." Father is coming to represent *men,* and she is becoming very much interested in men. He can teach her a great deal about men that will be very valuable to her. Most of all, he can teach her to feel a wholesome affection for men.

Sometimes, girls who have always kissed Father on the cheek or forehead now want to kiss him on the lips as they see Mother do. One girl who had kissed her daddy freely for some time decided to give him one of the Hollywood variety. Her father broke it off quickly and said, "Don't ever kiss a boy that way on a date." "Why?" she asked, looking surprised. "Because he may think it means you're leading him on." "Oh, Daddy!" she exclaimed, giving him a little slap on the cheek. But she never tried to kiss him that way again and she probably would think twice before responding to a boy who tried to kiss her that way.

Father can prepare her for many of her dates by taking her places himself. If she has an invitation to go rollerskating the following week, Dad might suggest that she try it before that time. She might invite some of her friends to go too, making a party. Father would have a chance to look the place over without seeming to be nosey, and daughter might be more "sure of herself" on her first skating date.

If son goes through the "woman hater" stage, father can be helpful to him too. When his son starts "making cracks" about women drivers and Mother's driving, Dad can say jovially, "Take it easy, son, that's my wife you're talking about." Or when the boy expresses irritation, or even hostility, toward girls, Dad can sow a good suggestion, such as "Lots of fellows your age feel that way. But in a year or two you'll probably think they're pretty nice. In fact, I'll not be surprised if you think a few of them are pretty wonderful." Meanwhile, Father can be a good listener, encouraging the boy to say why he thinks he feels as he does. Often we get the picture of a boy who lacks self-confidence or has had rather rough treatment by some girl whom he liked, and who is "afraid to stick his neck out" again. "Girls surely can be nasty at this age," he can be assured. "But as they get older they want boys to like and date them, so they learn to be pretty nice."

If children have known real love during their adolescent years, they will seldom settle for less in courtship and marriage. Because they have been loved, they will have learned to respond by giving love. There are always more people seeking to be loved than are able to give it.

Really loving young people means caring about them as well as caring for them. This means accepting their need for *self*-respect and *self*-confidence. They desire and need the respect of those they love, but because they are immature, their elders often lack confidence in them. This absence of trust causes them to lack confidence in themselves, and to act just that much more cocky and immature. Who is to break this vicious circle? Faith in their children is one of the greatest heritages parents can give them, for then the children are more likely to have faith in themselves.

"But how can one trust them when they show such poor judgment?" a mother asked her daughter's counselor. "What do you mean by poor judgment?" she was asked. Her daughter had previously told her counselor, "No matter what I do my mother always sees it in the worst possible light. It hurts me. What can I do to make her have more confidence in me?" Are we disappointed because our children do not act like adults? Are we hostile because they want to try out their own ideas instead of accepting ours, ready-made? Are we afraid to allow them to make mistakes and learn from the consequences? Were we made to suffer too much for our own mistakes?

These are difficult questions and there are no easy answers. This is particularly true in the area of sexual development. Mistakes are too costly. Perhaps if children are allowed more freedom to experiment in other less dangerous areas, they will not have so much need to assert their right to try out their own ideas regarding sex. The groundwork of parent-child-adolescent relationships is being built from birth onward. If parents give their children the love they need to feel wanted and appreciated during the early years, if parents have confidence in their ability to grow "in stature and in wisdom and in favor with God and man," that confidence will guide them through the experimental teens. Knowing they are loved, and therefore trusted, they will not need to bargain for affection, for they already have it.

Self-Esteem—Related to Sex Feelings

"What you think of you is one of the most important things about you," a counselor told a group of young people. This is equally true for adults. If they lack self-confidence and self-esteem, it will be difficult for their children to have confidence in them, or

[129]

esteem for them—or for themselves. The courage with which adults or children face a particular task or life itself, is determined by self-confidence, self-esteem. "I'm not worth a dime," sobbed an alcoholic. As a child he had had plenty of ability, but through the years an overly critical father had finally convinced him he was no good. "I could never do anything to please him," he said bitterly, "but my brother was always perfect." His sense of disappointment with himself and with life could be numbed only by alcohol.

"My fourteen-year-old was driving me crazy," one mother wrote. "He didn't seem to care how he looked. Every morning before he left for school I had to check to see that he had on a decent shirt, that his hands were clean, and his hair combed. I was nagging him, and I knew it was wrong. But I didn't know what to do about it. I couldn't let him go off looking as though he had no mother," she continued. "That night after your lecture on the importance of praise and affection, I got to thinking on the way home. I couldn't remember when I had praised him for anything. When I got home I questioned my husband, and he couldn't remember praising him for anything either. We decided that he probably needed approval and that we would look for something to praise. We had to look hard, for we remembered *flattery* wouldn't do the job. You said that praise was deserved appreciation but that flattery was 'an attempt at manipulation.'

"But when we really looked for things to appreciate we found there were lots of little things we had just been taking for granted. I thanked him for making his own bed, and Dad thanked him for putting the tools back after he used them. As we looked for things to appreciate, we found more and more things to praise. He began to improve, and we could honestly praise his improvement. He has just been coming along wonderfully. The other night we had a guest for dinner. Without any prompting from me our boy got all cleaned up and came down to dinner in a nice white shirt, and with his hair neatly combed. I was proud of him, and after the guest left I told him so. 'You know,' I told him, 'when you get yourself all slicked up, you're a very handsome young man.' 'You're a pretty slick chick yourself, Mom!' he said to me."

Naturally the mother was pleased. We all like to be appreciated, and we appreciate the person who appreciates us. We are critical of the person who is critical of us. But in this story, who had reversed the cycle of criticism and turned it into a cycle of appreciation? This mother. By appreciating her son's good qualities, efforts, and achievements, he came to appreciate her too. And that is exactly what a family should do for its members.

There is an interesting sequel to this story. A few months later, this attractive mother attended another lecture by the same psychologist. Afterward she spoke to him and recalled the incident above, and then commented, "My son has been kissing me goodbye when he leaves for school lately, but this morning he tried to kiss me right on the lips the way he sees his father do. Should I let him?" she asked.

Actually, this is quite a significant sequence in the development of love-sex feelings. A frustrated fourteen-year-old, unable to get *appreciation* had bid for attention by negative behavior. It was a poor substitute, for it gave neither mother nor child a sense of satisfaction. When his mother expressed genuine appreciation, he felt loved, and he responded by kissing her before leaving for school. Since she was treating him with more respect, he felt more grown up. And so he wanted to express affection for her in a more mature way, as he saw his father do, rather than the "childish" peck on the cheek. This was a high tribute, but she had refused him! Why? Fear? After talking about the possible reasons, she felt differently. It was a passing phase, lasting only a few days.

Perhaps, too, he was experimenting with making love. At fourteen, he had probably fantasied kissing a girl many times. Perhaps he wanted to practice a bit on his mother. One parent reported a "kissing bee" between her thirteen-year-old son and ten-year-old daughter. The family was driving along in the car, and the children were talking about a movie they had seen the night before. "This is the way they kissed, isn't it?" the girl asked her brother, and gave him a long kiss. They giggled and tried it again and again before they tired of the play. "We didn't know what to do, so we just ignored it," the mother concluded. "No, it hasn't recurred."

Our great-grandfathers and great-grandmothers would have been embarrassed if their children ever saw them kissing each other. Now, open affection between parents, and between parents and children, is encouraged. It seems to teach them that love is not limited, that there is plenty for all, and no need for jealousy. The more love we give, the more we have to give. The "taboo on tenderness" is a thing of the past. From here on it is hoped that any genuine expression of love feeling between parents and children, and between children, will not only be tolerated but appreciated, for from such experiences can come loving adults.

Loving is also expressed in appreciation, particularly appreciation for the child's need for self-esteem. "You're too nice a boy to do things like that," is replacing the "shame on you," approach. And "We know we can always count on you to be honest with us," builds self-esteem, whereas "I don't believe you" destroys it. Only as parents have self-esteem can they give it. They cannot give their children what they do not have. Fortunately, even if parents do not have it, they can build it if they realize that they have done the best they can. All humans do. It can be the hope of parents that they can increasingly give their children the affection and appreciation needed for wholesome growth.

Girls with too little self-esteem are likely to fall for the fellow who knows how to use flattery. They may seek attention by dressing to accentuate their sexuality rather than their femininity. "The way some of these girls dress, they look as if they had been poured into their clothes and someone forgot to say 'when,' " a high school boy commented. "Yes, and when you look at a girl that's dressed that way, you don't think of friendship, love, and marriage," another added. Girls who dress provocatively also often flirt in that way and neck with almost any boy who takes them out. They think they are popular, but often they are getting notoriety, not popularity.

In contrast, the girl who has an abundance of love is more secure within herself. She is not likely to become so boy crazy, nor to become boy crazy so young. She can dress to accentuate her features, not her figure. Liking herself, she can like boys, not use them. And liking boys she can express honest affection for them which is not so likely to be misunderstood. When a boy gets out of line she can draw the line and still let him keep his self-respect. "What have I done to give you the impression that I'm that kind of girl?" often brings an apology and real admiration. Being more secure in her ability to win love when she is ready, she is not in such a hurry to go steady, to become engaged, to marry. Time and maturity are in her favor, and she uses them to good advantage.

The boy who has never as a youngster proved his ability to win love, seems in many ways to be even more of a problem than is a girl in that situation. Never having experienced the satisfactions of being loved enough, he is likely to center his drive on ego satisfactions and sexual thrills rather than striving to win love. He is likely to strive for *power over* girls rather than *companionship with* them. Instead of *loving people* and *using things,* he gets the pattern reversed: he uses people and loves things. (Some women are that way too, of course.) As soon as he can, he may drop out of school and get a job. With his earnings he first buys a car, for with this car he can date. And it is in his car that he is most likely to feel the surge of power—*power over* the more than one hundred horsepower under the hood, and *power over* the girl at his side. All boys dream of this sort of power, naturally. But with the love-starved boy, it can become an obsession, a desire to which all else is secondary. Alcohol may increase his sense of power and is also at times a substitute for love. Taken in conjunction with a powerful car, or with a gang of other love-starved adolescents, it can spell trouble. Parents whose teen-age boys are mixing gasoline and alcohol should seek help immediately, not waiting until the newspapers list a child of theirs among the casualties of a head-on crash on Highway 84 at 2:00 A.M.

Unreasonable "conceit" is not really an exaggerated sense of personal importance, but just the opposite. Because a person does not *feel* important to anyone, he has to *act* important. Because no one has seemed to love him as he is, he tries to act as if he were someone more important, stronger, older, more powerful than he feels himself to be. These qualities threaten parents, and they are likely to react with hostility. Just the opposite is usually needed— more acceptance of the boy as a person, more love for him as he is, and better understanding, for he does not understand himself. It often helps to do more things *with* him, not *for* him.

There are some boys and girls who are starved for affection and for a sense of personal worth who do none of the things listed above. They merely withdraw from family and social relations as much as possible to avoid further hurt. As a substitute for real love and real achievement, they dream about them. Unless they are coaxed from their "shell" with love and successes, they may become more and more shy and withdrawn.

Fortunately, parents need not feel overwhelmed or helpless if problems develop. Understanding teachers, school guidance personnel, Family Service and Child Guidance agencies, the people who lead the church groups and youth groups in the community—all these can help parents if parents turn to them. Seeking help is not the mark of a parent's failure but the evidence of a parent who cares enough. Everyone needs help and benefits from it at times. The teen-ager who becomes a problem, is the youngster whose problems are not solved.

What Can Parents Do?

Whether we like it or not, adolescence is the period when the boy or girl develops strong attachments outside the home. Many parents unconsciously resent this and resist it. Instead, they would be wise to encourage participation in a good "gang"—first, of one's own sex, and later, a mixed group.

Since girls mature earlier, they often desire to take the initiative in getting the boys into a mixed group. Parents might well encourage them rather than feeling that they are being "forward." Male initiative comes later. A mother might suggest a home party herself when her young daughter and a girl friend are trying to think of things to do. "Why don't you invite two other girls so there will be four, and then just invite four fellows? You don't have to invite them for any particular girl." If the fellows asked are the choices of the girls, there will probably be a fairly natural pairing off at the party. A set of square-dance records and a phonograph will help. A popular TV show interspersed during the evening, and some "eats" (double portions for teen-age boys) to wind things up—and the evening should be a success. The girl who learns to be a good hostess is likely to be popular with both sexes.

A church group is one of the most natural and wholesome of the mixed groups. Everyone is welcome, and cliquishness is at a minimum. Adults who are interested in youth, some of them highly trained, are skillful in helping young people have wholesome fun together. Youngsters who enter the group primarily for the wiener roasts at the lake, the "overnights" at the church cabin, the Friday night folk dances at the social center at the church, remain to worship with the group. Under the encouragement of the leaders, they learn to accept committee responsibilities, and eventually, the leadership of the group. Boys and girls grow into competent adults not by accident but through a series of growing responsibilities. Parents who understand their children's developing needs are willing to make many adjustments and sacrifices to make appropriate experiences available when they are needed. Children grow up only once, and they will all too soon be on their own. These early teen years are as important in their way as the earlier childhood years of which we have heard so much.

We may need to stimulate more avenues of normal relations between the sexes, particularly during the high school years. Some high schools are experimenting with folk and social dancing, co-educational badminton, volleyball, and co-ed swimming, in addition to the usual band, orchestra, and dramatics. Four-H groups include both boys and girls. The YMCA has an excellent program with adult leadership to give Hi-Y boys a sense of belonging to a "gang." The Boy Scouts have a parallel program. The YWCA, Girl Scouts, and Campfire Girls have groups of a similar nature. There is a growing and highly commendable tendency to arrange co-ed functions between boys' and girls' groups.

Teen-agers without something to do are like fish without water. Is it enough for parents to encourage their own youngsters to participate in groups? Do they not need to be concerned that groups be available to all children in the community? Otherwise, youngsters themselves will form "gangs," and these unsupervised groups are the ones most likely to get into trouble for lack of something better to do. It may mean that parents themselves will need to accept responsibility for youth leadership. If they like and understand youngsters, have learned to make suggestions in question form rather than giving directives, this is not so difficult a task as many fear. Actually, it can be great fun.

In helping younger teen-agers plan their activities it is well to keep in mind that boy-girl relations are very important at this stage. The emphasis should be on activities which make it easy for them to change partners frequently and easily. For example, boys will enter into a "grand march" followed by a "Paul Jones" mixer type of dance before they are ready to dance a whole dance with one girl. A boy fears "getting stuck" with some girl with whom he is uncomfortable. He does not know how to "get rid of her" at the end of the dance, so he avoids asking her. But a directed dance which starts and ends with the boys on one side of the room and the girls on the other will find the boys much more enthusiastic participants. For the same reason, square dancing, in which there is a frequent rotation of partners, will be more popular with most boys than social dancing.

By the same token, parents ought not to discourage a frequent change of boy friends or girl friends by accusing young people of being "fickle" or "faithless." Change is the order of the day or in fact of the age, and is to be expected. The truth is that at this age youngsters are so absorbed with their own problems that they are not very considerate of each other's feelings. Irritation with each other, plus a smile from "someone new," is sometimes enough to bring about a change of boy friends or girl friends. A friendly "Well, who is the boy friend just now?" may make it easier, not only for them to change friends, but to tell the parents about their new friend.

These changes also bring a certain amount of heartache, for the boy and the girl seldom decide to change at just the same time. Usually one is left stranded by the other and feels rejected. Casual assurance that this may be expected at this age may be helpful. Likewise, a few questions as to what might have irritated the other youngster, may help the deserted one to avoid the behavior later. Often they can see, too, that it is their pride that is hurt. They were really both getting tired of each other, and he or she, too, now has the chance to make some new friends. For parents to be interested in what children tell them helps the youngsters to feel that someone loves them, and merely talking about it makes them feel better. Learning to ask the questions that help teen-agers accept the situation and think of constructive things they can do, may save them much unhappiness. "Does there have to be anything wrong with either of you, or could it be that you just don't suit each other? Isn't that what dating is—to find out the type of person you most enjoy?" are examples of the kind of questions that can be asked.

A few boys and girls will stick together almost from the first. This may indicate that they are both unusually mature and thoughtful youngsters who get along well with almost everyone. On the other hand, they may be "clinging vines" who tend to hang on to someone they have, rather than "fly to other ills they know not of." In any case, a reassuring and relatively hands-off policy is the safest for parents. As indicated earlier, boys and girls appear to show uncanny insight in choosing someone who meets their needs. Perhaps everyone does, and that is why marriage is such a popular institution.

CHAPTER 8

Helping the Adolescent Become the "Right Person"

Parents almost universally want their children to marry happily. Their youngsters normally have the same desire. Many problems that arise are the result of different conceptions of how to achieve that goal.

Finding—or Becoming—the "Right Person"?

Boys and girls today grow up in a rapidly changing culture. Most girls come into adolescence with a great concern about being romantically attractive. Getting a husband at the conclusion of a whirlwind romance is impressed upon their minds from the time they start going to movies. The entertainment world thrives on this romantic stereotype. Advertising stimulates and cashes in on the same stereotype to sell goods. To be sure that she is prepared for that great moment when "the right man comes along," so that she will elicit "love at first sight," the girl must be sure that at all times her hair is kept neatly in place with an "Allure Home Permanent," her lips must be kept inviting with "Kiss Me" lipstick, and her curves must be kept seductively proportioned by a variety of bras, girdles, and other previously unmentionable articles of dress (but now blazoned forth from almost every page of our magazines). Social approval has been substituted for self-esteem as the basis for ego satisfaction.

Meanwhile the fourteen-year-old boy is probably car or sports minded. Sure, he is flattered by the flirting of the girls, but he takes it for just that, something to take or leave as he sees fit. Having a girl is not a necessary part of the development of his masculine ego; being able to "take it or leave it" does contribute to his sense of power over the other sex. As he moves on into high school, however, and dating seems more and more the thing to do, he may become increasingly involved. As a rule, when he dates, he tends to be attracted to a younger girl with whom he feels equally experienced, or possibly slightly superior.

The boy, too, is exposed to the romantic myth. In the typical movie boy meets girl and they fall in love at first sight. They have to fall in love at first sight—only an hour and a half is allowed for the whole show. Then a series of problems is introduced to entertain the audience and hold it in suspense. But, in the end, true love triumphs, and the movie ends with a passionate embrace and the implication that the couple will live happily in a state of delicious insanity forever.

The typical movie romance, however, when played out in real life, by real people, often ends in a real divorce. What is the effect upon young people's attitudes when they grow up on that kind of emotional diet? What do parents teach them that counteracts this romantic nonsense? Can they blame the motion picture producers for giving people what they want? Whose job is it to teach children that people *grow to love* rather than *fall in love?*

If parents are willing to give up the "romantic myth," youngsters will do so more readily. Is it honest to tell their sons and daughters, "When the right person comes along, you'll know it"? Is that perhaps wishful thinking on the part of parents—no fuss, no muss, no bother? Is it not more realistic to teach them that a happy marriage is not so much the result of finding the right person as of *becoming* the right person; not of falling in love, but in *growing to love?*

In helping their children *grow to love,* parents must recognize that there will be a growth of sex feelings too. They do not help their youngsters by ignoring or depreciating sex feelings, any more than by perpetuating the romantic myth. "It became increasingly clear to me, as you spoke, why my first marriage failed," a young woman told the marriage counselor. "I married quite young, and I can see now that I married for romance and he married for sex. We weren't really seeking the same thing, and we separated within a year." Neither had married *to give love*. She had mistaken romance for love. He had mistaken physical attraction for love.

One of the important phases of sex education is to help boys and girls, men and women, understand their own and their partner's sexual nature. A girl may not realize that the romantic thrill she experiences as "love" is in part a *generalized* sexual response. The boy, on the other hand, may have as strong feelings of love as she has, but he is more aware of the highly *genitalized* feelings aroused by intimacy. A clear understanding of this basic sex difference would do much to improve the love relations between the sexes—both before and after marriage.

Out of this basic difference much confusion may arise. To the girl, each date may be a test of her ability to attract love. So, probably unconsciously, she invites "loving" from the boy; yet, if the boy is a bit too aggressive, she is frightened. Even as late as her freshman year in college, one girl wrote of her problem: "I must be terribly confusing to boys. I even confuse myself. If a boy tries to kiss me on a date, it makes me furious. If he doesn't, I wonder what's wrong—doesn't he like me?"

Part of this girl's confusion is due to the boy's feelings, of which she is almost completely unaware, and partly to her own feelings which she does not really understand. If the boy is tenderly affectionate with her, she is thrilled and feels wonderful because she thinks this is proof that she is an attractive woman who can elicit love. But to the boy this same intimacy is very exciting. To her, their kisses are a beautiful expression of affection; to him, they are apt to be just so much "fuel under the boiler." She interprets his excitement in terms of her own feelings of loving and being loved. He interprets her ardor as a projection of his own passion rather than as affection. He may "get fresh" and get slapped. Her feelings are hurt that he should think her "that kind of a girl." His feelings are hurt, too, as well as his masculine ego, when his ardor is repulsed so violently. And yet he admires her for having standards. In some cases he feels he has been led on and then repulsed. From the high school girl you may get the question, "I enjoy necking with boys, but why do they always try to get sexy?" Ten years and two marriages later she may say to the marriage counselor, "I love to lie in my husband's arms and make love to him, but why does he always have to get so sexy?"

Failure to teach girls to understand the sexual nature of the male is to court confusion and trouble. Can they be taught to recognize sex feelings in themselves and in the other sex and learn to avoid situations which stimulate sex apart from love feelings? How can parents reinforce their children's teen-age idealism that intercourse should be reserved for marriage where it can be a true expression of love? Can they teach their boys and girls the danger of confusing physical attraction with real love, marrying, and finding they have little in common upon which to build a marriage? Can parents help them find creative outlets for sex tensions during the adolescent years? How can more emphasis be given to psychological attractions *before* marriage and physical attractions *in* marriage?

Infatuation is an ego, rather than a love or sex reaction. It is often called "puppy love," for it *can* grow into the real thing. But the high school boy guessed well in his speculation on puppy love: "I guess it's all right for kids, but if you get married on puppy love, you'll probably lead a dog's life." Infatuation is more nearly self-love than love for another person. Here is a girl who has had very few dates. She is not sure just how she rates. Then a boy comes along and treats her as though he thinks she is wonderful. It makes her feel wonderful. So she thinks he is wonderful. Actually he has just made her feel more certain of her own attractiveness. And that is all right, for it increases her self-esteem. She may think she is in love with him, for in the nature of human interaction, we tend to like the person who makes us like ourselves. This makes it easier for us to grow to love each other. To be able to love others *as* ourselves, we need to love ourselves first.

Parents should never ridicule an expression of "love" for a certain person, even when it is obviously "puppy love." "I'm glad you like Jim," the parent might say. "I hope you'll continue to feel that way. But at your age you shouldn't be surprised if it tapers off. Most of us think we're in love a number of times before we finally settle on the person we marry. Take your time, for time is in your favor." Or better yet, the parent asks questions which help the girl to reach that conclusion herself.

The Importance of Dating

In the last half century, our society has developed a characteristically American process of getting young people married. It is a process of dating, going steady, getting serious, becoming engaged, and finally getting married. Each stage serves an important psychological function. If young people go through each stage in an orderly and mature fashion, their chances of a happy marriage are greatly increased. Dr. Henry Bowman felt that "hurry" was the cause of most of the divorces he studied. In over half the cases, young people had married too early, had not known each other long enough, or had not had a long enough engagement—one or more of these factors was responsible for the failures.

Some parents act as if dating were a necessary evil, to be postponed as long as possible and limited as much as possible. They are anxious because they hear of young people who have become involved and "gone wrong." They forget that the vast majority of youngsters take this period in stride, carried along by their own self-respect, genuine adolescent idealism, and a concern about their future happiness in marriage.

At the other extreme are those parents who rush their children into dating too early, and force them beyond their depth at almost every stage of their development. Both sets of parents miss the main point— the social and emotional growth of their youngsters.

Studies show that there is a wide variation in the normal ages at which young people begin dating, become engaged, and marry. About half the high school boys and one-third of the girls "seldom date." One-third of the boys and one-fifth of the girls do not date by the time they are seventeen. Yet half the girls are married by twenty years of age, and half the women who have not married by age thirty will still marry. The wise parent relaxes and attempts to offer guidance rather than to direct his youngster's dating activities.

Double and group dating should be encouraged. Being in a group of four does not make so many demands on each individual as when there are only two. There are four to help make conversation, four to help keep activities social rather than sexual—providing all four have constructive ideas for good things to do. As it was indicated earlier, small groups in homes satisfy most of the values to be gained from dating, and reduce the hazards of unsupervised single dating. As one girl put it: "Any girl can neck, but if you're really smart you don't have to. There is always something better to do if you can think of it." Talking frankly with sons and daughters about the sexual versus the social side of dating, and causing them to think of constructive things to suggest is helpful, providing parents *ask* them what they might do, rather than *tell* them what to do. "How would you like to bring some of your friends here after the dance for sandwiches and chocolate?" "Has the gang ever thought of organizing a party at the church after the game? Wouldn't Mr. Jones help you?" They may not act on the suggestions immediately, but a month later, they may pop the idea on the gang just as if it were their very own.

All young people need limits. A time to be expected home is a good idea. Even college girls admit that it has saved them from some "drip" as often as it has cramped their style. No one wants to be the one to say, "Isn't it about time to go home?" Young people need parents to be scapegoats: "I've got to go—my mother says I have to be home by twelve." It is usually fairly easy to compromise on a time beforehand. Parents and daters both need to know when the party, dance, or show will be out, how much time must be allowed for eating or whatever "the other kids do," and what time they are expected home. Hostesses make it easier all around if they invite youngsters to a party "from nine to twelve"; dances should let out at a given time; even church parties need a scheduled hour and a statement that "refreshments will be served." If anything happens so that young people cannot make it by the expected time, they can call and let their parents know when to expect them. Seeing that they have money to make such a call (or to come home by bus or taxi in case the girl should have a quarrel with the boy friend), or promising to reimburse them if they spend their own money, will encourage them to keep in touch with their parents.

A deadline also helps a girl to avoid sexual involvement. Long-continued intimacy tends to become more arousing. Fatigue also tends to reduce resistance and dulls the ability to make decisions. Encouraging young people to start and end parties earlier makes sense. They should not expect to keep up with or outdo the college or young adult crowd. When parents keep reasonable hours themselves it makes it easier for teen-agers to accept the idea that to stay out half the night is not necessarily a mark of being grown up.

Dating is important, too, in teaching the "social know-how" of getting along with the other sex. Most young people need to learn what is really expected and desired by their dating partners. Both boys and girls are likely to think that "popularity" is very important, but college students at least say they prefer someone who is "natural," good-natured, and considerate. Boys tend to think a car and money are more important than girls say they are. On the other hand, girls tend to think boys expect more affection than boys say they expect. For example:

"Should you kiss a boy on your first date?" This question is asked by teen-age girls more frequently than any other. The old answer, of course, was a resounding "NO." The counseling approach would suggest instead that we ask in reply some pertinent questions:

1. "What do you want a kiss to mean?" There was a time when a kiss was reserved as an expression of affection. A girl did not kiss a boy until she was

very fond of him and wanted him to know it. At one time that first kiss was almost tantamount to an engagement. What does it mean now?

2. "Why would you kiss him, if you did?" Because he expects it? What would lead him to expect it? Would either of you be kissing for a sexual thrill? Will he think you don't like him if you don't kiss him, or will he respect you if you refuse in a friendly way? How would he feel if you said, "I don't think it's fair to a boy to kiss him until I know him well enough to know that I really like him and want him to know it?" What would it mean to him then when you did kiss him?

Studies show that youngsters who have "self-assurance"—knowing you know how to act and knowing what is right or wrong—rate very high with teen-agers themselves. Wide dating experience, at the right time and of a wholesome nature, helps a youngster to gain this self-confidence.

Going Steady

Winning the right to choose their own marriage partners, as part of a developing democratic family pattern, youth has continued to experiment with various patterns of courtship. At first, dating was permitted only to engaged couples, then to those who were serious about getting married, and more recently, dating has been extended downward to even relatively young children who think of marriage only as some distant future event.

One of the intermediate stages young people have developed has been that of "going steady." For some, it is almost the only form of dating they know—that is, going with only one person at a time. With others, it represents a progression from "playing the field" —wide dating—toward a centering on the most likely candidate of the moment. Going steady has often disturbed parents because they consider it this latter form and feel their son or daughter is too young to be getting serious. Young people themselves will debate hotly the advantages and disadvantages of going steady. Because it means one thing to one group of young people, and something else to another, it is important for parents to find out what "going steady" means to their own child at the time. It may change in a few months, so we need to keep informed.

Some junior high school youngsters use the term in the way we used to talk about having a boy friend or girl friend. It may not even be dating, but just smiling at each other, and walking from class to class with each other. In some cases, the other half of the "steady" couple may not even be aware of the relationship. The other girls were talking about their "steadies," so Mary told them John was her steady— which meant she *wished* he were her boy friend. Usually going steady means that two young persons are dating only with each other.

Girls are likely to be more interested in going steady than boys. If a girl is dating anyone who asks her, she has to wait until a boy invites her. But if Ruth is going steady with Joe, she can say, "Why don't you come on over tonight and we can do our math together and watch television?" Girls brought up in the American pattern to feel that they are just as good as boys and with the same rights do not fit easily into a pattern which gives the boy the entire initiative, and in which he expects her to accept his invitation to do what he wants to do in the way he wants to do it. Slowly but surely, a dating and court-ship pattern based upon dominant males and submissive females is changing. Perhaps the earlier tendency to go steady is an adjustment which makes the dating relationship a more mutual arrangement almost from the start. Looking at it in that light, some parents might feel differently. Most of them do not like the idea of their teen-age daughters being "submissive" to the adolescent boy.

Boys who are ready to go steady, do so for a variety of reasons, some of which they recognize, some of which are probably unconscious. Boys will say frankly that going steady is cheaper. They can have more dates on the same amount of money. They take the girl out sometimes and sometimes they can have a pleasant evening at her house or at her expense. This may be good unless it permits them to be together so much that they soon tire of each other.

The shy boy, who is not sure of his ability to get dates, or to win approval and affection, finds it much easier to ask a girl who has already accepted him than a girl who might refuse him. He is never quite sure whether the reason a girl gives him for refusing is the real reason, or an excuse because she does not want to date him. And some girls can be downright cruel. Certainly parents should teach their daughters to refuse a date with real consideration for the boy's ego. He is probably not nearly so sure of himself as she is. If she would like to date him again, she might say, "I'm sorry I can't make it (and give him the reason if feasible). I hope you'll ask me again very soon." If she is genuine in her feelings, he will not be hurt and he probably will ask her again. Maybe, too, girls should be encouraged to help boys who need help rather than just avoiding them. "I'm sorry, Joe, but frankly, I don't like to date boys who want to neck all the time," she might say. If more girls refused a second date with boys who had shown them little respect on the first one, and told them why, both girl and boy would probably benefit. At least he would know why she said, "No," and would not worry about having "B.O." or fear that the girl was embarrassed to ride in his jalopy.

There are some dangers to going steady that should be considered. When a couple start going steady, they really indicate to other prospective dates that they are not interested in them. Unless the couple have both dated widely enough to know that they have more in common with each other than they do with others, they may be shutting themselves off too early from wide dating experience.

There is also the problem of breaking up. If a couple start going steady too early and before they are mature enough to make the adjustments that a continuing relationship demands, one or the other, or both, may get on each other's nerves and break up. If they have a good scrap and tell each other exactly what is irritating them and both break off at the same time, it is not so bad. But if one walks out on the other, the rejected one may be "heartbroken." It helps for them to understand that being left high and dry does not necessarily mean there is anything wrong with them. The time may come, when boys and girls are so considerate of each other that rather than walking out on their former "steady," they will encourage some other boy or girl to date her or him or will even arrange a blind date for her (or him).

Sometimes young people hesitate to break up when they have really lost interest because they don't want to hurt the other's feelings, or because they fear they may not have dates with others if they do. Occasionally they just "get in a rut" and keep going together, becoming a couple of clinging vines who are afraid to let go, at the same time resenting, unconsciously, their dependence upon each other. They may even go on and marry, still resenting each other but feeling secure. Such marriages usually do not end in divorce, but neither is there much happiness in them.

By far the greatest danger of going steady during adolescence is the growth of intimacy that occurs naturally with continued association. Remembering that girls during this period want most to be assured of their lovability, and that boys get an exciting physical reaction from intimacy, one can understand why the situation is charged with possible misunderstanding. Unless a couple consciously limit physical expressions of affection for each other to a few goodnight kisses, and other fairly fleeting contacts, there is likely to be a rather steady growth of physical contact and physical response. Because of the generalized thrill that intimacy brings to girls, and the genitalized thrill it gives to most boys, youngsters are naturally tempted to experience it again and again. One of the frequent and disturbing questions that come from teen-agers is "How far can you go without going too far?"

It is this tendency for the sex impulse to grow under repeated stimulation which has caused the great fear of this powerful drive. Either we control

[159]

the impulse to repeat the experience, or the increasing stimulation comes to control us. If a couple start out doing a good deal of necking, there is a strong tendency to move on to petting and real sexual arousal. If they allow this to continue, enjoying the thrill and feeling confident that they can draw the line short of intercourse, they may be surprised to find that for human beings, as for transatlantic flights, there is a "point of no return." This tendency toward a build-up of desire, coupled with the feeling of growing "love" on the part of the girl, bringing with it the desire to give joy to the person she loves, causes many young couples eventually to "go all the way."

Many other couples, of course, knowing of the dangers, limit their physical contacts from the first. An evening of dancing, followed by parking and petting, creates more tension than most young people find comfortable. Sometimes this tension, in itself, causes one or the other to break it up. Sometimes, as with one girl, that first momentary impulse to "give in" was such a jolting experience that she resolutely broke off with the boy. When she agreed to go out with him again, several months later, she was a more mature and wiser girl, and took much more initiative in suggesting activities that involved a minimum of physical contact. They did more hiking, swimming, and playing tennis—less intimate dancing and necking. If parents can make clear to their youngsters that because physical intimacy stimulates the sex urge, as well as the love impulse, they must learn to guard against too much physical contact too early, then one of the strongest arguments against going steady can be eliminated.

Another danger is that teen-agers may translate this physical attraction as intense love feelings, be convinced that they are madly in love with each other, and want only to rush into marriage at the earliest moment. Finishing school, waiting until they can finance a marriage, and other reasonable considerations may seem to them secondary at the time, so strong is their attraction. Having ideals that do not permit premarital intercourse, but realizing that they are flirting with "the point of no return," they must hurry into marriage so that their intimacy may be legalized. Even when the boy is soon to go into military service and they will be separated for a year or more, they feel almost driven to fulfill their sexual intimacy. (Incidentally, a brief period of marriage before a long separation may make the separation more difficult for both of them than if they had maintained a less intimate relationship until they could enjoy a real marriage.)

A group of young people voiced the opinion that there was real value in going steady because it helped you to "really get to know a person." "The first few times you go out with a girl," one boy said, "you are both so busy putting on the big act that you don't get to know the person as she really is. Only after you've gone together a few times, and begin to relax, do you get to see the real person you've been going out with." The others agreed. What they were actually saying, is that one's first reaction is an ego reaction—to make a good impression. One may be irritated by this pretense on the part of the other, or flattered by it, and feel mildly superior. Helping young people to realize that when they try to impress someone they usually give the wrong impression and that they make their best impression when they are genuinely *interested in getting to know the other person,* should do much to relieve the anxiety and self-consciousness of first meetings and first dates. This could prevent, or at least reduce, uncomfortable self-consciousness which in turn would improve the quality of dating. Thus one reason for going steady could be eliminated.

If parents can also reduce or delay the need to go steady by seeing that their boys and girls have the opportunity to belong to a mixed group where the youngsters know each other and circulate freely; if they can help teen-agers to feel self-confident and secure enough to play the field a little longer; if they can make it possible for them to realize the danger of growing physical intimacy and to learn to keep relationships with the other sex on a more friendly and social basis, then they will probably discover that going steady is a desirable and natural stage in the development of the maturing relationship between the sexes. If young people also know that it is natural for such relationships to be tentative and temporary during the early years, much "heartbreak" and ego damage can be prevented. In other words, if the idea can be de-emphasized that people "fall in love" and the idea instead be taught that truly *growing to love* is a challenging task that requires time, young people will probably make their transition from childhood to adulthood with much less turmoil—and so will their parents.

From Dating to Courtship—Getting Serious

These stages are not clear-cut and distinct. The previous section explained how excessive physical attraction may be mistaken for intense love feelings, producing a premature seriousness about marriage. In an earlier discussion of infatuation another type of premature seriousness was dealt with.

"How can you tell when it's really love?" This question is asked again and again of anyone who attempts to help youth with this problem of *growing to love* a member of the other sex. And the answer is not simple. When one gives up the simple certainty that goes with the belief in a "one and only" and "this is the one," then one must rely, to a considerable degree, on reason. But loving involves feeling and does not readily yield choice to reason. One counseling service, designed to bring together mature people with common interests, backgrounds, achievements, religion, disbanded after six years. Bringing together people who "logically" should be ideally suited to each other was apparently not the answer. "In six years of operation, we never succeeded in marrying off an engineer," the social worker commented. "They came to us with a set of specifications, and expected us to find the perfect wife for them. They couldn't seem to realize that a happy marriage was not the result of *finding* the perfect mate, but of *learning to love* someone who wasn't perfect."

Another reason logic alone fails, is that apparently, choice of a marriage partner involves to a considerable degree the selection of someone who can satisfy often unconscious emotional needs. Though people are normally not fully aware of these needs as they operate in themselves, they *can* become more aware of them and at least use them as an aid to reason in selecting a marriage partner.

Parents cannot expect to select their son and daughter's partners for them. But perhaps they can help the children to be more "reasonable" in that choice if they can learn to ask good questions—questions that will set them to thinking more realistically about their own and their prospective partners' needs and expectations. Parents, too, can provide experiences which will give them a broader basis for judgment.

"My daughter wants to take her boy friend along up to our summer cabin for a couple of weeks," a mother complained. "I'm afraid that if they see too much of each other they may decide to drive on over to Reno some day and just get married, and I'm quite sure he is not the man for her. I'd hate to see her do anything foolish that she'll regret."

"Oh, ye of little faith," thought her daughter's counselor to whom she had taken her problem. After an hour with the counselor, the mother's basic faith in her daughter's good sense triumphed, and she was willing to try the *test of companionship*. With real cordiality she invited the young man to join them in the mountains. Before the first week was up, her daughter was bored stiff with him, and he, sensing the mounting tension, left for home with some lame excuse.

Often parents, lacking confidence in either their son or their daughter, or in their "heart throb" of the moment, try to separate them. They send daughter across country or overseas, hoping the long separation will cause them to forget each other. Sometimes it works, if their attraction has been primarily physical. As often as not, they write romantic letters to each other, and "absence makes the heart grow fonder." Correspondence romances are not to be trusted.

Instead of separating them, it is wiser to try to bring the couple together in a family setting. The girl can be encouraged to invite the boy friend frequently for dinner and a quiet evening at home with the family. The more she sees him in a family setting, the better idea she will have about what kind of husband and father he will be. If she sees him only on dates, she will know only what kind of escort he is. Observing how interested he is in younger brothers and sisters, and how he gets along with them, gives clues to his real attitude toward children. Encouraging a wide variety of physical activities, such as hiking, swimming, tennis, gives them a chance to see each other under many conditions.

"What can I do?" a distracted mother asked a counselor. "My daughter has never dated and had the experiences other girls have. She was always overweight until a short time ago when a medical examination showed she needed thyroid. After she lost fifty pounds, the boys began to date her. At the USO she met a young Air Force cadet and fell madly in love with him. Now they want to get married during his furlough this month. She's twenty-one, but this is the sort of thing that should have happened to her at fifteen or sixteen. And yet, if I persuade her not to marry him now, and something happens and she never marries, she might always hold it against me. What can I do to slow her down and make her more reasonable?"

The counselor helped her to realize that if she could ask the right questions, her daughter might see the wisdom of proceeding more slowly, and so they discussed some of the questions she might ask. "What does he plan to do for a living after he gets out of service?" "What kind of student was he in school and how likely is he to succeed in making a reasonably good living for you and the children?" "What do you know about his family?" "Shall you enjoy his family and be proud to be a member of it?" and similar questions. The mother reported back several weeks later that it had worked. Her daughter was to go with the boy to visit his family in another state during his furlough instead of getting married. After the furlough, during which her daughter and his family had gotten on famously, his parents drove them back, met her family, and together they made plans for the wedding—several months later on his next leave. Everyone felt happy about the marriage when it occurred.

When parents can ask good questions, they can be genuinely constructive in helping their young people to make wise choices. But the important thing is the spirit in which the questions are asked. If the questions are asked, for example, in an attempt to get the daughter or son to wait another year because the parents would feel better about it, then the questions will be resented. No one likes to be manipulated. But if young people feel that their parents are on their side and are trying to help them discover reassuring evidence, rather than finding fault, they will often welcome help—and equally important, they will feel that their parents really care about them and their happiness. Feeling secure in their parents' love, they will be more able to give love and less likely to grasp for it.

"Pinning"

"Pinning" is for half the girls and three-fourths of the boys "being engaged to become engaged if and when things work out so that we can marry." But for half of the girls and one-fourth of the boys, it is a real engagement. Some plan to buy an engagement ring later; others plan to get just one ring—a combination engagement and wedding band. Girls take pinning more seriously than boys. The important point is that the two involved be clear about what the step means to them.

Others tell of a corresponding pattern among the nonfraternity and out-of-college youth. In some cases the boy gives the girl a ring, but not a diamond ring, to be worn on the third finger of the left hand. Or he may buy her a nice wristwatch, or some other substantial gift, to indicate that he is more than a casual friend. In some cases they exchange gifts by prearrangement which constitutes a tangible proof to each other, their families, and friends, that they are growing very serious about each other.

In an increasingly mobile culture like ours, with more young people going away to college, into the services, to the city to find employment, being transferred to other communities by the companies that employ them, pinning may serve a very real purpose. Often now, young people become serious about someone they have not known long and neither one may know the other's family. This new intermediate stage of "declared seriousness," but lacking the finality of an engagement, may give them a new freedom to get to know each other's family, and see the other in his family setting, which was lacking in so many of the war marriages and postwar divorces.

Pinning or its equivalent should make for greater clarity of feelings and of goals too. There are some things that are none of one's business until committed to a serious concern about another person. With this mutual expression of seriousness, a wall of uncertainty is leveled, and it becomes easier to explore together the real concerns each has for future relationships.

Becoming Engaged

As pinning or the giving of a watch or some other needed or desired token of real seriousness becomes a more common practice, many of the adjustments that previously took place during the engagement period will be fulfilled before the engagement is announced. The engagement period itself may become shorter but more final. We would expect to see fewer broken engagements, with the embarrassing sense of failure they so often bring to the couple. Actually, they ought not to be thought of as failure at all. If the couple discover that they have not grown to love each other enough to give them reasonable assurance of a happy marriage, it is certainly wise to postpone the wedding or to break off entirely. The attitude of parents and friends probably ought to be, "Aren't they wise and courageous to break off now rather than go through with it and then face the more difficult readjustment of separation or divorce? Far better to find out now that they don't love each other than after they marry and have children!"

"If it's really love, I shouldn't have any doubts, should I?" one girl asked with real concern. Obviously she believed still that when the one and only man of her dreams came along she would *know* he was the one. For people who *think*, as well as feel, there will probably be some periods of doubt until the wedding itself. Deciding who and when to marry are two of the most important decisions a person ever makes, and the price of error is considerable. It is only natural that a person should wonder at times whether he is acting wisely. There is no cause for real concern unless the periods of doubt increase in frequency and intensity as the date of the wedding approaches. In this case, it might be well to suggest that a young person consult a religious or psychological counselor. Sometimes just verbalizing these doubts releases them. Sometimes verbalizing them focuses the intellect upon factors which need further clarification.

Most states now require a blood test prior to the granting of a license to marry. It is recommended that instead of this minimum required by law, a complete medical check-up be sought. Parents owe it to their children and to the young people they are marrying, to make sure that they are as well prepared for the long journey ahead as medical science can make possible.

It would seem wise too, if feasible, to consult a gynecologist, a physician who is specifically trained in understanding feminine sexual functions and who could be counted upon to do a thorough pelvic examination. Such an examination can do much to reassure the bride-to-be regarding the condition of the hymen, the normality of the clitoris and vagina, and her capacity for sexual union. The gynecologist is better prepared than most physicians to answer any questions either one may have regarding their anticipated sex life. The physician may suggest, on the basis of muscle tone and other symptoms, treatment that will not only improve general health but aid in the problem of sex adjustment. (See section on "Physical Factors That Help" in Chapter 10 which deals with sex adjustment in marriage.)

The formal announcement of the engagement should commit parents to give every emotional support to the forthcoming marriage. They may have "been against the marriage from the first," but if their efforts to head it off have not worked, and the couple have set the date for the wedding, the parents are morally obligated to swing to the support of the marriage and do everything within their power to help it succeed. If they do not, and the marriage fails, they share the responsibility for that failure.

Space does not permit a discussion of planning the wedding. Duvall and Hill in *When You Marry* have a whole chapter of suggestions for anticipating this event. Less extravagance and more sincerity, less formality and more simplicity would make for less nervous exhaustion and more rested brides. In some social groups, weddings have become so expensive that conscientious young people are often tempted to elope to save their parents the heavy costs. This procedure would deny them, their families, and their friends the joy of sharing together in the traditionally gay occasion of a wedding. It is good to make something of a marriage, for it is indeed an important event, but it need not be an extravagant occasion. Some young people are exercising the courage to forego the elaborate wedding and reception (which some brides have dreamed of ever since they were flower girls) and are seeking group approval by making their wedding simple but "different." If ever there is an event in a couple's life together when they should feel free to plan a service that will be meaningful to them, it should be their wedding. Big formal weddings differ only in the cast of characters and the amount of money spent. Many couples act as though the wedding were the celebration of a long-sought goal. Actually, it is the beginning of a serial story—a story in which a man and a woman continue to grow to love each other more and more, as they journey down the years, hand in hand.

In Summary

Growing to love is more difficult and time consuming than *falling in love*. It demands more maturity and mutuality on the part of the young people. It requires more assistance and guidance from parents—yes, and more tolerance and understanding, too.

But parents will be rewarded if they can encourage their young people to mature as loving and appreciative human beings, capable of giving love to, and eliciting love from, the person they eventually marry.

CHAPTER 9

Sexual Freedom—Real or Imaginary?

*E*very human being is a bundle of psychological needs and desires. His behavior is largely determined by them. Many of these desires conflict with one another, hence there are certain paradoxes of everyday living. For some individuals, the desires for immediate physical pleasure is dominant. For others, the long-range desire for a successful and satisfying marriage is the value to which other desires are subordinated. Parents, almost universally, hope their young people will choose the long-range desire. Most young people feel the same way. But how much do they know of what is involved?

Freedom—Not License

In the simple authoritarian societies of the past, young people conformed to the patterns laid down by preceding generations. Modern American youth, brought up in an atmosphere in which learning to make choices is considered more important than conformity, expect more freedom of choice in sexual matters too.

Freedom, however, is not synonymous with happiness. Freedom is only the "right to choose"—wisely or unwisely. How can adults help youth to realize that freedom is not license to do as they please, but to choose—and live with the consequences?

Home, school, and church once set the patterns of social acceptability. Now youth are bombarded by a variety of stimuli so that they might well think, "This is a new day—anything goes." But where does it go?

Children today grow up in groups where many youngsters are immature, self-centered, and exploitative. Helping teen-agers to be aware of the kinds of behavior which stimulate the development of mature love feelings, as opposed to those which stimulate sex feelings apart from, or mistaken for, love, helps them to direct their behavior toward desired ends.

They are also constantly exposed to misinformation and wrong attitudes. "Should youth be denied sexual intercourse, which is not only harmless but necessary, during the most passionate years of their lives? This may create in them harmful repressions which damage their personalities." This is the exact quotation of a question handed in by an eighteen-year-old girl for group discussion. Would parents want their sons or daughters to act upon the gross misinformation implied in this question?

The confusion exhibited here is similar to that of many persons who glorify extreme permissiveness to the neglect of essential discipline. Many parents, for instance, overreacting against the once commonly held idea that it was a parent's duty to "break a child's spirit," go to the opposite extreme. They are afraid to restrain their children's behavior lest they "repress" them. What happens? Are their children happy? Are they "free"? Is not discipline (firm support and guidance) as surely needed for healthy growth as is opportunity for spontaneous expression? It is *why* an impulse is checked and *how* that makes for harm or for health.

To inhibit means "to check, to restrain." As such it is good, and enables us to make choices. Every time we make a choice of action, we inhibit all but one of the possible impulses and act on that one. The term "repression," on the other hand, is usually employed to describe an unconscious choice, with certain possible responses being automatically ruled out because of fear or guilt-producing experiences. Used in this sense, repression is often harmful, since it limits our freedom to make conscious choices.

A boy passes an ice cream parlor and thinks how

good a chocolate milk shake would taste; but he wants to make the team and so he reluctantly passes it up. He has made a conscious choice. He has blocked an impulse. But suppose he had been conditioned early to feel that eating anything that was not necessary for health was to be a glutton. Feeling guilty about wanting a milk shake, he might not even admit to himself that he wanted one; in other words, he might repress the impulse. In this case, he is not aware of what is controlling his behavior. He may feel angry without knowing why.

A child overtaught to *fear* crossing the street on his way to school, may have a panicky feeling every time he crosses a street, years later. A girl, made to feel that sex is vulgar and disgusting, may find herself unable to really enjoy the sex relationship, years later, in marriage itself. Not knowing why she feels as she does, she may experience the frustration that results from her basic desire to respond and from her *repressed* feeling that sex is vulgar. Unconsciously, she may project this hostility against her husband and thus increase marital conflict.

If, on the other hand, a girl is motivated, not primarily by fear, but by a deep desire to become a warm and affectionate wife and mother, her response can be voluntary and positive. If she is aware of the intricate relationship of love-sex feelings, she can more easily check the expression of impulses which would not contribute to her ability to feel and indicate genuine love for a member of the other sex. We block some impulse every time we make a choice—dozens of times each day. Providing the choice we make gives us either immediate or long-range hope of greater satisfaction, frustration and resentment are reduced.

The girl quoted above apparently failed to recognize that one might inhibit the sex impulse—as indeed most young people do—for good *conscious reasons*. One suspects that there may also be a strong element of rationalization in her statements. Most behavior results from a number of motivations acting at the same time. In trying to explain their behavior, people learn early to select the reason that seems most acceptable and try to persuade themselves and others that this is *the* reason that they want to do what they want to do.

The words *repression* and *rationalization* are not important in themselves. The behavior they describe is important. Understanding this behavior can help to free parents and children to guide their feeling, thinking, and behaving more satisfyingly.

Some of the most confusing choices regarding sexual behavior come to young people when increasing feelings of love cause them to desire greater and greater intimacy with the loved one. Even if parents have kept the channels of communication open with them during the adolescent years, they may know little about one of the paradoxes facing their children —namely, the desire to give increasing love without going "too far" and violating their own, and society's, moral standards. The important thing is that they know parents really care about them and their happiness. Here again incidents that occur in the community, or are reported as occurring elsewhere, can be utilized to seek with young people long-range solutions to some of these problems.

"How Far Can I Go Without Going Too Far?"

One of the teen-ager's main concerns about sex is how far he can go without going too far, for in this concern he expresses the realization that to become capable of really loving another person, and to win a responding love from that person, requires the growth of intimate feelings. The more we like a person the more we want to express affection. But between biologically mature young men and women, this intimacy also normally stimulates the sex urge. Young people are therefore faced with the necessity of learning to be affectionate without becoming so sexually involved as to "go too far" (as teen-agers themselves label it).

Here again they show wisdom, for they are not ready, for the most part, for total involvement. They need time to get to know each other well enough in many situations, before they can be sure that this person is the one with whom they want to share their life. They need, too, to grow up emotionally and intellectually to the place where they can cope with the other than love-sex problems which marriage brings. Helping them, through experience and discussion, to realize that marriage is more than a love-sex union, that it involves educational, vocational, economic, and other responsibilities, helps them to deal more realistically with the time factor, and not to become involved too fast, too far, too soon. They learn that even the giving of affection must be controlled in terms of long-range goals.

For some girls, apparently, this question "How far can I go . . .?" covers a fear that boys know some tricks or "techniques" by which they can sweep a girl into sexual intimacy against her real desire. Helping girls to realize that they themselves are sexually aroused normally only with fairly continuous physical contact and stimulation enables them to lose their fear of any affection giving, but to draw the line at continuous or prolonged kissing and petting. Learning to be a good conversationalist and keeping the conversation on less intimate topics is one technique many girls themselves have discovered. Boys find it hard to get "amorous" with a girl who is chatting gaily about the last dance or the next football game

—and even harder when the topic under discussion is some national or international problem or some problem of religion or philosophy.

Boys, too, would be wise to learn to keep the relationship on a less intimate level. The boy's "point of no return" is usually reached sooner than the girl's. More than one boy has suddenly found himself sexually involved with or married to some girl he would not have given a second thought to a few months earlier.

Is There Such a Thing as Sexual Freedom?

A high school senior poses a problem. "I became engaged about a year ago, and a short time later persuaded my girl to begin intimate relations with me, since we were going to be married eventually. In the last few months she has become more and more demanding and disagreeable, leading to frequent quarrels. Recently I suggested that we break up. She says if I leave her now, after having had sex relations with her for a year, I'm a heel. I don't want to be a heel, but neither do I want to marry a girl I don't love. What shall I do?" Is there really such a thing as sexual freedom? For whom? The interplay of sex, love, and guilt feelings narrows the limits of sexual freedom as surely as any external controls.

The important question for young people, for parents, and probably for society, is this: "Does premarital intercourse contribute to, or interfere with, successful courtship and marriage?" In some cases apparently, love feelings are intensified, and the relationship culminates in marriage. In others, just the opposite appears to take place. In a great many cases, intercourse puts a strain on the relationship. Because of the insecurity of the relationship and the possibility of pregnancy, the drive of the average girl toward marriage is increased. At the same time, the drive of the male toward marriage is often reduced. Marriage means new responsibilities and, at least unconsciously, many men avoid those responsibilities as long as possible. The insistent and persistent sex urge is one of the reasons for marrying. As long as he can satisfy his sexual desires by frequent intercourse his reaction to "When are we going to get married?" may well be, "What's your hurry?" Seeds of doubt may begin to grow in her mind. "Does he really love me, or am I just being a sap?" she may ask herself.

Interestingly, he too may begin to wonder whether he really loves her or whether she is a "sap"—and for a very interesting reason. From childhood forward, but particularly during adolescence, sex talk, "sexy" stories, and the like tend to divide women into two groups; those who "will" and those who "won't," those who are "naughty" and those who are "nice." Sexual fantasy is usually associated with the former; love fantasy, with the latter. When the girl "gives in," during courtship or even during the engagement, she may be unconsciously moved from the group who "don't" to the group who "do," with a consequent change of feelings about her as a woman to love.

Typical of the change of feeling some men experience was the young man who told a marriage counselor, "I'm graduating from college in a couple of weeks, and a week after that we're planning to be married. But the closer I get to it, the more jittery I get. Is that natural? Or does it mean that we shouldn't get married?" The counselor said that some uncertainty was natural but suggested that they begin at the beginning and talk it through. The couple had been going together for almost two years, and had been engaged for the past year. Gradually, during recent months they had begun having more frequent and more intense quarrels—over little things. "How long have you been having sex relations?" the counselor finally asked. "What makes you think we have?" the young man asked in surprise. "I've found in the past that this type of quarreling is often associated with the strain of premarital intercourse," he replied. Somewhat embarrassed, the young man admitted that they had been having intercourse for several months. "Had she ever had intercourse before?" he was asked. "She said she hadn't."

"Did you believe her?" "I did then." "What do you mean, you did *then;* don't you now?" "Well, frankly, I don't know," the young man replied. "She gave in to me."

A year before, these two young people had faith in each other. They became engaged, and looked forward to a marriage. Then a few months before, under his urging, they had "gone too far" as she explained it in a subsequent interview. After that there was more conflict on dates, he urging intercourse and she resisting, but finally giving in. "I began to wonder whether he really loved me or just my body," she concluded.

A rising tide of doubt had almost submerged their love feelings. "She seemed to have lost faith in his love for her, and he had come to doubt whether she had been a virgin," the counselor summarized the case for a little group of counselors who met regularly to discuss their cases anonymously. He concluded that after several conferences during which their doubts had been verbalized and their basic faith in each other, and in their mutual love, had been sincerely expressed, the marriage was performed as scheduled.

A woman counselor then raised the question as to why the matter of virginity seemed so important to men. "Your question reminds me of an illustration used by a philosophy professor when I was in college," one of the group replied. "He was trying to force the students to distinguish between *knowledge* and *faith*. Some of the students insisted that it was just a difference of degree. He insisted that to be happy we need to "believe" some things that we could never "know." For example, he said, 'a woman knows it's her child; a husband can only have faith it's his.' We roared," he concluded, "but I'll bet none of us ever forgot the point he was making."

"Your story reminds me of a young father I was asked to counsel last year," another commented. "I had been given several instances in which he had been unreasonably harsh with his six-year-old son. I was trying to help him analyze his actions in these situations and to discover why he had acted as he did. 'I suppose the real reason is that I'm not sure he is my son,' he said bluntly. The boy had red hair and there was no red hair in either his or his wife's immediate families. There were red-haired relatives on both sides, but even a discussion of recessive genes did not seem to reassure him. So we looked into their early relationships. He had had sex relations with his wife before they were married, and he knew of other fellows who had had too. He readily admitted that he had had intercourse with numerous other women before marriage, and a few since. I asked him if he thought she had had intercourse with any other man since their marriage, and he said that he thought she had, but he could offer no proof. Suspecting that he might be projecting his own guilt feelings on her, I asked him if he thought it was wise to feel this way when he had no proof, particularly when he himself admitted having had adulterous affairs. 'Well, maybe not,' he said, 'But at least she knows they're her kids, and I don't know they're mine.' "

"If I Should Become Pregnant He Says He'll Marry Me"

Surprisingly, in some groups in America, pregnancy is a common pathway to marriage. The men in these groups seem to feel no particular devotion or loyalty to the woman, but to the child. They feel the women are as responsible as they are, and can look out for themselves. But if a woman becomes pregnant and cannot work, then someone must care for her and the child. Does he stay married after the child can be "parked with relatives" or is old enough to go to school? In some cases apparently a lovable baby stimulates love feelings in both mother and father which radiate to each other and the marriage "works." In other cases, the sense of responsibility for both mother and child is temporary.

In still other cases, men who have professed their love and loyalty want to head for the nearest abortionist when pregnancy occurs. Some women take this as a rejection of them personally (and of their child), and as calloused unconcern for their health and future welfare. They become bitter toward such men—and men in general—which makes it more difficult for them to let themselves love another man later without damaging reservations.

In many cases one or the other resents being forced into the marriage. Americans resent dictation, even by situations. There is a tendency for each to try to escape guilt feelings by projecting blame on the other. "If you hadn't insisted on having intercourse, this wouldn't have happened." "If you had been willing to get married in November instead of waiting until June so that you could have a big wedding, things would have been different." In some cases the woman is "just sick" about becoming pregnant, and this psychological illness, coupled with pregnancy, makes the period an extremely unhappy one, instead of one of elated expectancy as for some women.

In one case, a woman came to get help in handling her child. She frequently lost her temper and spanked her one-year-old; then she would be overwhelmed by guilt feelings. Talking out the hostility which she remembered feeling about her premarital pregnancy seemed to help. She had hated her husband at times before their hasty marriage and during her long period of nausea. She remembered having had strong feelings of guilt and had sensed the embarrassment experienced by her family, though they had been wonderful about it. There had been periods of depression during which she considered moving to another community—and she had even contemplated suicide. She still resented the hurried civil marriage, rather than the wonderful wedding she had always planned. Aided in understanding the past and guided toward some new interests, she felt better. With help, she improved her relations with her husband and other people in the community. She was gradually able to accept the situation, and her child, and a year later she entered happily into a second pregnancy.

A second case presented startling similarities, except that the mother "parked" the three-month-old infant with relatives and went back to her job. When the child was about a year old, this woman began having such pronounced periods of depression that she sought medical and then psychological help. After a period of analysis she was able to accept and talk about her feelings for her child, her husband, her marriage, and her long-range values. At this stage she decided to stop work, and "be a full-time mother and wife," as she put it. A short time later, she too, voluntarily sought a second pregnancy.

These two women were thousands of miles apart and of different races and cultural patterns. Yet their reactions to forced marriage were so similar as to be startling. In one case the husband was loving and supportive; in the other he had entered into an affair with another woman which complicated but did not wreck the marriage. The difference in the husbands' attitudes did not seem to affect the women's attitudes as much as might have been expected.

Intercourse for Engaged Couples?

It is true that engaged couples have greater freedom to be together than non-engaged couples. We recognize their desire to be alone with each other to talk about future plans. We recognize their need and desire to visit more freely in each other's homes to get to know the family they are about to marry into. Since 87 per cent of the women who had experienced premarital intercourse had it with the man they later married, and, as Kinsey's data point out, a considerable portion of the intercourse occurred during the year or two before marriage, it would seem that much of the premarital sex experience of women occurs with the man they are eventually to marry, in their own homes. Or was it that they became engaged or got married because of love or guilt feelings created or intensified by intercourse, or by pregnancy? We cannot tell from the data.

Forty-one per cent had intercourse with both the man they later married *and* other men. Some of these were probably engaged to the "other men" at the time, since apparently only one-half to two-thirds of all engagements end in marriage. Why do from one-third to one-half of all engagements break up? Reasons given in interviews and on questionnaires are not always the real reasons. Counseling experience would indicate that sex is often a factor. In some cases, sex attraction or intercourse rushes a couple into an engagement which does not work well, so they break up. In other cases, tensions arising out of too intimate petting, intercourse, or disagreements over whether or not to have intercourse break up an otherwise workable relationship.

Take, for example, the couple that had been acquainted for a long time, had gone steady for a year, and then became engaged. Lately, nearly every date had ended in a quarrel. "The next day one or the other of us calls up and apologizes, and we make up. Then on the next date it happens all over again," the girl complained. A few questions by the counselor brought out the fact that they thought any intimacy short of intercourse was all right for engaged couples. They agreed they wanted to save intercourse for marriage. What they were not aware of was the build-up of tension that was being created through physical contact and the frustration of the aroused drive that expressed itself in irritability and quarreling. When they saw the alternatives, they readily decided to reduce the amount of physical contact. They found that not too difficult, and the tensions were reduced.

In another case, a girl sought counseling because following each of the last three dates with her fiancé she had started to cry while preparing for bed. "I couldn't stop. I wasn't unhappy, but I just sobbed and sobbed until I finally fell asleep. What's wrong with me?" she asked. Questioning revealed a situation similar to the one just discussed, and the crying stopped when the intimacy was reduced.

But, some might ask, if they had intercourse would this not reduce the tension and prevent conflict? If both experienced satisfaction this might be true. Then, however, tensions over guilt feelings or conflicts over the frequency of intercourse might arise. Some say that if there is real love and consideration intimacies may produce not friction but marriage. Others insist that if there is mature love both would prefer to wait. Some groups sanction premarital intercourse for engaged couples. But most Americans still think it is unwise and that it detracts from the real significance of marriage itself.

Mutual Love or Exploitation?

Almost half, 46 per cent to be exact, of the married women in the Kinsey sample who had premarital intercourse had it only with the man they later married, and another 41 per cent had intercourse with the man they married as well as with other men. This makes it clear that "promiscuity" is limited to a relatively small group of girls or women. For most women premarital intercourse would seem to involve at least some elements of love, since 87 per cent of them married either "the" man or "one of the men" with whom they had had intercourse.

The same cannot be said for men. According to Kinsey (Volume I, page 557): "In some cases, lower level males may have intercourse with several hundred or even a thousand or more girls in premarital relations. There are quite a few individuals, especially of the grade school and high school levels, who find more interest in the pursuit and conquest, and in variety of partners, than they do in developing long-time relations with a single girl." Such individuals exemplify exploitation rather than love.

The word "mutual" would seem to hold the key to the meaning and effect of premarital intercourse. If intercourse is mutually satisfying, there is normally an increase of "mutual attraction." As this attraction increases, the desire to repeat the experience increases. Marriage is the social arrangement worked out by society over thousands of years of experimentation as the one in which these intimate love-sex feelings can be most naturally and spontaneously, and mutually, expressed.

Terman's earlier study in California indicated that those who married the only man with whom they had had intercourse before marriage were apparently as likely to be happily married as those who had not. Those who had had additional premarital experiences were not. True mutuality during premarital affairs would seem, in fact, rather rare. In the matter of orgasm, for example, almost 100 per cent of the men achieve orgasm every time, whereas only two-thirds of the women *ever* achieve it. What starts out as the expression of, or the seeking for, affection on the woman's part becomes for him sexually stimulating. She is then put in the position of either withholding affection and breaking off the intimacy and facing the possible irritation of the man, or of giving in as a complete expression of her love for him, hoping that it will bring forth mutual feelings in him. She believes his verbal expressions of love because she feels that way, and she wants to believe he does too. Aroused, she may gamble everything on her ability to win love, or on the fear of losing it.

The male, at the moment of sexual arousal, becomes a bundle of contradictions. Sexual arousal pours adrenal secretions into his blood stream, and his emotions and sex urge take over. He "loses his head," as an old phrase describes the process by which reason surrenders to passion. His reactions are those of a person in shock, anger, excitement, or intoxication, and his judgment and statements are just about as reliable.

Fortunately, however, men can be *humanized* by

love. If the ability to love, to care about another's feelings, has been nurtured since childhood, the heightened emotional reaction accompanying sexual arousal is contained within a framework of love. The basically shy boy is encouraged and proposes. The conscientious boy who had planned to wait until he could better afford to marry is "swept off his feet" and asks the girl to marry him—soon. The young man who has not been sure makes up his mind. <u>The most important decisions of life are probably made with the emotions, more than with the intellect.</u> They will be based upon love, sex, fear, adventure and faith, in varying proportions. Which emotions will be dominant?

Judson Landis reports (pages 134-135) three studies made in 1940, 1947, and 1952 involving almost 4,000 students in thirteen colleges and universities throughout the country that show surprising agreement. Approximately three-fourths of the college women, and half of the men advocated premarital chastity. Only one girl in twenty-five and one boy in eight recommended premarital sex experience for both men and women. An interesting shift of opinion occurred between the women of the 1940 study and those in 1952. Twice as many of the 1940 group gave as their reason for refraining from intercourse "the fear of pregnancy," while twice as many of the 1952 group gave as a reason "fear that sexual relations will stand in the way of marriage." "I want to wait until married" was the answer most frequently checked by both men and women in the 1952 study.

In the past, we have depended largely upon fear to inhibit the sex urge—fear of pregnancy, venereal disease, social ostracism. But we have not always utilized the most justifiable fear of all—the fear that too much emphasis upon sex may prevent the development of mature love, may even cripple the individual's ability to love.

How *mutual* then is premarital intercourse? Do both persons involved have the same desire or urge? Is it equally satisfying to both? Do they share equally the risks of pregnancy? Do they share the nausea and the birth pains if pregnancy occurs? Are their love feelings equally intensified? Are both equally motivated toward marriage? Why then do we have such phrases as "masculine conquest" while we refer to girls as "giving in"?

Some would insist that the women have their reasons or they would not "give in." They hope to win love, or fear losing it, so they allow the generalized sex feelings to progress too far before they put on the brakes. Others, they say, have intercourse in order to get attention, dates, companionship, recreation, social recognition. Still others say "giving in" roots in insecurity, and that some girls actually seek pregnancy since in their group pregnancy brings marriage and at least some degree of economic security and social acceptance.

Some Useful Ideas

"Will our children have the willpower to resist when temptation comes?" This question, phrased by one parent is felt by us all. To the degree that we have confidence in our children's ability to make wise decisions we can be less anxious and more relaxed with them. "My mother always trusted me. It just wouldn't have occurred to me to let her down," one student wrote in an autobiography. Many echo a similar theme. In contrast was the sexually delinquent girl who told the clinical psychologist, "My mother was always suspicious of me. She was always accusing me of having sex relations with boys, so I decided I might as well as long as I was going to be accused of it anyway."

"I know we can trust you to do what you think is right" seems to be a helpful approach. Too many parents try to impose upon their youngsters their own standards of behavior. Teen-agers have their own standards, and they draw the line at different places than parents do, but most of them are fine and idealistic. Youngsters get into trouble not so much because their values are wrong as because they do not live up to them. Giving them confidence in their own ideals, and encouraging them to live up to them is more effective than attempting to impose ours on them.

"I know we can count on you to act in a responsible way," is another good phrase. "I appreciate your taking responsibility for the younger children (or the animals, dishes, or whatever) when I needed your help." "We know that we can count on your being responsible for your own behavior," and similar statements give our youngsters that sense of responsibility that tips the balance when emotional or sexual arousal makes decisions more difficult. Marriage is the public announcement by two persons that they are prepared to accept personal responsibility for each other and for any child that may be born to them. If young people are ready to accept responsibility for sexual behavior, they normally prefer to marry and have society's approval and support. If they are not ready to accept the responsibility have they a right to be intimate?

" 'Don't ever have sex relations with a girl you wouldn't be happy to marry if you had to,' was a phrase that helped me," one man recalled. "When I was tempted to have sex relations with some sexy number, I found myself asking that question, 'Would I be happy about marrying her? How would my family feel about having her in the family?' That usually cooled me off considerably. The girls I would have been happy to marry wouldn't let me get to first base," he concluded. The same approach apparently also helps girls. "Would you be happy to marry him? Would you be proud to have him as the father of your children?"

"A Hi-Y leader helped me," another young man commented. "He asked us fellows during one of our discussions how we would like to marry a girl who had had sex relations with a lot of fellows. Most of us said we wouldn't. Then he asked us whether we had a right to ask for something we could not offer ourselves. That thought always helped me," he continued, "because I wanted to feel that when I found the girl I wanted to marry I was good enough to look her right in the eye and ask her to be my wife. I wanted to marry a fine girl, and I wanted to feel I was as fine as she was," he concluded with conviction.

"I think that's about the way I felt," another added. "Someone gave me the idea that I should plan for a marriage that would last fifty years, and get ready for it. When you look at marriage that way, it makes it easier to wait a few more years."

A young Navy V-12 cadet was having a chat with his chaplain during the war. Finally he got around to the subject of sex. "There is so much talk about sex in the barracks that it is hard to keep your mind off of it," he commented. "You wonder sometimes if you're losing out on something—if you're just being a sap to hang on to your ideals." "Well, Frank," the chaplain asked him, "do you think it would solve your problem if you went out and chased around the way some of the fellows do?"

After a few moments' silence Frank replied. "No, it wouldn't, would it? As a matter of fact, it would probably make it worse. Actually, there are fellows over there flunking out of their chance to become officers because they don't study. All they think about is sex. The more they think about it, the more they chase around. The more they chase around, the more they think about it. It gets to be a vicious circle, doesn't it? I guess the best thing for me is to decide what I want to do with my life and how I can best use my energies right now in that direction." Frank aspired to being a surgeon some day, and in the months that followed, he discovered that the positive channeling of his energies into his studies was the answer to his sex problems—not fighting aroused desires.

Girls seem to be helped by the realization that "it's the woman who pays." Men seem to be able to separate sex and love in a way that is impossible for most women. Some men will enter intercourse with any female they can persuade—or pay—to do so. The physical thrill which motivates his behavior is not affected by the way such a man feels about the girl. Actually, apparently the more he cares about the girl the less likely he is to urge intercourse before marriage. With the girl, it seems just the opposite. The more she likes a man, the more she wants to please him. The more intimate she becomes, the more her love-sex feelings involve her with him. He may break off the relationship with little emotional concern. Not so the woman.

Second, society expects the girl to set the standards and determine the limits of the relationship. As a rule, her sex drive is not so urgent, nor so easily aroused as his. And she has an inhibition he does not have which comes from the fact that "it is the woman who bears the child."

If the relationship does not end in marriage, again it is the woman who bears the emotional brunt. If she becomes convinced that she has no respect or love for him and breaks the relationship, she is likely to be disgusted with herself for having "been taken in" by his smooth line or hypocritical love-making. If he breaks the relationship, she feels rejected. If she marries him, she may have doubts as to whether he is really in love with her—or with sex. But if she can win his love without the aid of sex, she will feel more confident of holding and enriching his love with the added enjoyment of a sexual companionship in marriage.

Some boys try to give girls the impression that "everybody's doing it." That is just not true. Three-fourths of the married women in Kinsey's sample had either had no premarital intercourse, or had intercourse only with the man they married. Intercourse for a physical thrill is apparently rare among teen-age girls, both because of the later development of orgasm capacity and because of teen-age idealism and romance.

Some girls find it difficult to answer the boy's challenge, "If you loved me as I do you, you would want to have intercourse with me." She can answer by saying, just as logically, "If you love me as I do you, you wouldn't want me to—you would want to save intercourse for marriage. What do you want *marriage* to mean—just a legalization of a relationship which has in fact been going on for some time? Or will marriage mean more if it is also the beginning of sexual intimacy and living together with the approval of our families and society?" If the marriage ceremony is only a legal ceremony will it mean as much, and be as permanent, as if it were also a religious and psychological "beginning"? Many a young couple who went "all the way" have regretted the incident which made a hasty marriage before a "J. P." necessary.

Some young people cite Kinsey's data to indicate that those who have premarital sex experiences adjust better in marriage. His data show no such thing —nor does he suggest it. His data reveal only that those who had experienced orgasm before marriage responded more quickly and frequently in marriage. What else would one expect? The more sexually responsive a girl, the more likely she is to "give in" before marriage and respond with orgasm in marriage. Remember, too, that the girls who had premarital intercourse without orgasm made a poorer showing during their first year of marriage than those who had no experience. Practically all studies have shown that as a group, those who enter marriage with no previous sex experience make a better *all round adjustment* to marriage than those who have had sex experiences.

One thing that helps girls to escape involvement is to avoid situations in which emotions are likely to get out of hand. Parking to neck in some isolated spot is something that the wise girl resists. If she permits it, the boy is encouraged to think she may go further. He may become more aroused and aggressive than he would if they had parked in front of her home. Incidentally, hold-ups and rape frequently occur in isolated surroundings. Nor does the wise girl invite her escort into her apartment or room alone or at night. Such action *may put ideas in his head,* even if they were not there before, and she may find him difficult—and difficult to get rid of at bedtime.

The girl who makes decisions in advance of emotional situations also has the advantage. "I realize now that my problem was that I never made up my mind in advance," one woman confided during a conference. "If a boy was really swell and sweet to me on a date, then I wanted to do something nice for him too, I guess, so I'd give in. But if he was too aggressive or sexy that would make me mad, and I wouldn't even neck with him." Her behavior was not determined by principles or ideals, but by the feelings and impulses of the moment. As might be expected, one of her affairs led to pregnancy and forced marriage. Before the child was a year old, her husband had deserted her.

Both boys and girls are helped by anticipating situations and deciding while they can be reasonable what they will do if the situation arises. It is also helpful to discuss situations with other young people, particularly when there is an understanding adult present to lead or stimulate discussion. Under such circumstances those who act on the basis of reason can state their reasons more clearly than those who operate on feelings or impulse. People who like to talk about sex and advance ideas of sexual freedom in bull sessions are likely to have the least to contribute to such discussions. Good discussion groups give moral support to the boys and girls with ideals when other teen-agers they admire speak out on their side of moral issues. Church and Y groups have helped many young people. Secondary schools, with teachers trained to lead vital discussions of these important sex problems, could make a real contribution too, for they would be able to reach many of those most in need of help.

The Relativity of Sexual Freedom

Sexual freedom is relative. We have more freedom of choice than in some cultures, less than in others. But in giving more freedom our group expects more individual responsibility. Youngsters need more "built-in controls" than in the days of separate schools for boys and girls, and constant supervision. In view of the very great increase in freedom made possible by the automobile and the passing of chaperonage, the relatively small percentage increase in premarital intercourse should increase our confidence in the self-control of modern youth. If we can give them the information and understanding they need to make wise judgments (for judgments can be no better than the knowledge upon which they are based), we can be confident they will increasingly weigh the risks against the satisfactions and, more importantly, take the long view and ask themselves what kind of marriage they want for the next fifty years.

Are they willing to behave for the next few years in the manner most likely to contribute to a lifetime companionship based upon maturing love? Will they feel that all the satisfactions and securities such a life can give will reward them for subordinating sex feelings to love feelings during the days when they are trying to choose the person with whom they can most enjoyably spend the rest of their life? Have we built in the idealism and the self-control that will aid them in making long-range choices? Has our own home given them the love, understanding, and self-esteem that will make them want a home very much like the one they grew up in?

The more successful we are in helping our young people to become warm and loving human beings, the more likely they are to respond to the love needs of others. This may mean earlier courtship and an earlier desire to marry. With educational and military demands cutting deeper into adult life, we may expect to see more married couples in college, particularly at the graduate level. There is evidence that married students do better than average academic work, even those with children, who seem to do the best of all. The problem may therefore be primarily economic, and those of us who aspire to both advanced education and successful marriage for our youth may need to prepare to share with them the economic problems involved. Parents once expected to give a dowry or "the north forty and a team of mules" to a young couple starting marriage. It may again become an accepted practice to help our young people enter marriage when they are psychologically ready rather than exposing them to the strain or intimacy of the long engagement.

CHAPTER 10

Love and Sex in Marriage

This chapter is written for parents personally and, indeed, for all married couples. It goes without saying that the parents' attitude toward sex—what they think and how they feel about it—influences their children's feelings more than what parents say. It influences, too, one's relationship with one's husband or wife, a most important factor in the child's home.

It is quite possible for happy, wholesome, normally effective individuals to grow up in the environment of homes where the sex relationship and the sex factor in the love feelings of parents are not anywhere near ideal. But it is also possible that a parent's attitude toward sex, in most instances, *can* become more creative.

Marriage—a Love-Sex Companionship

Many people come to marriage with unrealistic expectations. Most married couples eventually work out fairly satisfactory adjustments. More than a few have found that if they can be more comfortable and honest with themselves and the way they feel, they can be more understanding of others and the way *they* feel. They discover a new freedom to reach out with love and imagination, to trust their feelings as well as their intellect, and to come closer to the individual with whom they are sharing their life and their love.

Marriage is basically a love-sex companionship involving body, mind, and spirit. Sex can stimulate and communicate feelings of love. "God is the author of sex, as of every other good thing," a priest told a group of mothers attending a meeting to discuss the sex problems of their teen-age sons and daughters. Not sex, but the wrong use of sex, was sinful, he reminded them. The use of sex to create families and to give stability to the family while the children were growing up was part of God's plan, and therefore good, he insisted.

Maturing of sex and love feelings should broaden the range of both. The husband who is affectionate only when he desires to arouse his wife sexually, usually finds he does not succeed. A woman wants to be loved first as a person; she wants to be sure her husband loves *her,* not sex. But if she doubts his love for her because it has a different quality from hers, she is limiting the range of love-sex feelings as surely as he would be if he felt that she did not love him merely because her sexual desire was not so strong as his.

Within the security and intimacy of a successful marriage, the range of love-sex feelings can continue to grow. One of the basic human needs, as was pointed out earlier in this book, is the need for adventure. This applies to sex, too. Though society does not approve of adventuring with a variety of partners, it does not discourage variety within marriage. A willingness to combine experimentation with "the tried and true" should keep a couple's sex life from becoming monotonous.

A satisfying prelude is more important to a woman than to a man, so the wife might well plan it. Encouraging her husband to "make a date" with her in advance gives her time to build up a psychological "readiness." (Many couples have some pet phrase meaningful only to themselves.) For some, an evening of dancing is a desirable prelude. For others, lying before the fire and listening to their favorite recordings or any one of countless intimate experiences, intensify their satisfactions in being man and wife—man and woman.

Spontaneity seems to be the watchword of the moment itself. Knowledge of sound techniques is all to the good, but water poured on a plant does no good until it seeps into the ground and comes up through the roots. The greatest satisfaction often comes when the woman abandons herself to her impulses and her husband makes every effort to respond to her subtlest wish.

A couple should feel free to experiment with a variety of positions. The old male-above position requires the man to assume a tense position of pelvic thrust which makes it difficult for him to delay orgasm. Dr. Rudolf Von Urban in his book, *Sex Perfection and Marital Happiness,* suggests an unusually relaxed position and approach that is particularly helpful for men troubled with premature ejaculation. Arden, in *Handbook for Husbands and Wives,* and Butterfield, in *Marriage and Sexual Harmony,* suggest a variety of positions which most couples find helpful.

Feminine Initiative

Feminine initiative serves several functions. First, it makes a woman equally responsible for the achievement of a satisfying sex relationship. Since she is the more difficult to arouse and satisfy and since she is the only person who can tell what is most arousing and satisfying for her, it makes sense for her to feel free to guide the relationship.

In taking the initiative, she assumes an active rather than a passive role. One young husband reported that after several months of marriage during which his wife had been completely passive, he got disgusted and broke off the relationship, explaining that if she were so bored he would go down to a certain tavern and see if he could find someone who would *enjoy* having sex relations. He dressed and left the house in anger, going to the tavern indicated. After some thought, his wife dressed and followed. She found him drinking a beer—alone. All she said was, "I'm sorry. I'll try to change." He went home with her but forced her to take the complete initiative. For the first time in her life she experienced orgasm.

A similar incident involved the discovery of infidelity. The woman loved her husband, but felt that she should leave him as a matter of principle. She wisely sought counsel. During the conference, she admitted to considerable disinterest in sex. She left the conference with the determination to win her husband back and a confidence that she could do it. That night, for the first time in her life, and after two years of marriage, she experienced orgasm. Active effort increases tension. Orgasm is the "break-

ing dam" and the flooding diffusion of tension followed by relaxation.

The Franks discuss the same problem in the section on "The Married Mistress" in their book, *How
to Be a Woman.* That unique feminine quality
which is a blend of love and sex entices many a man
to marry and keeps him happily married. He could
stay in his own home and continue to be loved by
his mother and he could hire a cook and house-
keeper or someone to care for the children. But as
the men's chorus in "South Pacific" expresses it,
"There Is Nothing Like a Dame!" During her courtship days, a woman's future is tied up with her
ability to be interesting to men. It is she who usually
initiates the cycle of interest and good feeling. It is
she who suffers most if she takes her husband and
her marriage for granted and then finds he has
turned to some other woman who is making an effort
to be interesting.

This is not to suggest that a woman pretend, but
a generation ago, two famous psychologists (James
and Lange) advanced the theory that if we *acted as
though* we were not afraid it made us less so (whis-
tling in the dark). If a woman acts on the faith that
the sexual side of her marriage can be pleasurable,
her husband will normally do his share to make it so.

Feminine initiative is not only stimulating to a
woman, but it is highly satisfying to a man. Because

of his more localized sex feeling and easier arousal, he is usually the first to be stimulated and aroused. If he can be patiently affectionate until she takes the initiative in suggesting or leading him on to further intimacy, he is made to feel that he is able to contribute to her happiness too. For centuries women were not supposed to experience any pleasure in sex. Intercourse was supposedly pleasurable only for the man. It was therefore one-sided and exploitative. The male received pleasure but did not give. Now, the normal mature male is delighted to give pleasure as well as receive. More than ever before, sexual intimacy can become a truly mutual experience.

This is probably as good a time as any to highlight a difference in sexuality which has not usually been recognized and utilized in a couple's mutual search for sexual adjustment. In the male the drive toward orgasm is predominantly physical, and the orgasm releases fluids which carry life-giving cells into the sexual partner. With orgasm, the physical urge is reduced, leading rather quickly to relaxation and the desire for sleep. Were man's desire only a physical urge, he would probably be content with intercourse once or twice a week, as indeed he may become after a period of marriage. But during the honeymoon period, at least, the novelty and excitement of this new intimacy is quite impelling. For this reason, if he is not wise, he may want to experience the intimate love-making, union, and orgasm as often as possible. Apparently, however, every situation, even sex, is dulled by overindulgence. This may be particularly true for the woman, especially if the man acts without due consideration for her feelings.

On the other hand, sexual desire and orgasm are, for the woman, "learned experiences." There is no evidence in other mammals, with one or two exceptions, of either intense female desire or orgasm. Orgasm serves no biological function in the female, unless the arousal and the flow of blood to the genital area increases the flow of sexual secretions which facilitate insemination and impregnation. But whereas orgasm in the male brings about a reduction in the physical urge and eventually in the physical ability to repeat the act, this is not true of the female. Sexual arousal for her may be cumulative rather than exhausting. If her physical responsiveness is above average and her desires selfishly motivated, she may actually desire intercourse so frequently that her husband, unable to satisfy her, develops a psychological impotence that is almost an exact counterpart of the frigidity often found in the wives of demanding husbands.

In other words, the more a woman finds genuine satisfaction, the more frequently she desires to be aroused. The more frequently the man experiences orgasm, the less his physical drive to orgasm. A realization of this difference and its utilization in achieving adjustment gives new hope that greater mutuality of sexual desire is not an impossible goal for two partners who are eager to contribute to each other's happiness.

Typical, for example, was the case of the minister's wife who came to a religiously oriented marriage counselor. It soon developed that the problem was almost entirely sexual. Her husband was oversexed, she said, and his constant demands were causing her to consider divorce, though she knew that this would be a very serious threat to him professionally. "What do you mean by *oversexed?*" the counselor inquired. "Just how often does he desire intercourse?" "He always desires intercourse and keeps trying to get me to give in to him," she replied. "How often do you have intercourse?" she was asked. "I think intercourse every week or two should be often enough," was her judgment. "Have you ever heard of the fellow who was always complaining to the man who worked at the next desk about his wife's constant demand for money? He was finally asked by the man what his wife did with all this money. 'I don't know,' he had replied. 'I never give her any.' You remind me of that man," the counselor said. He then described the nature of the physical—and psychological—urge in the male and suggested that she change her tactics and not only acquiesce to his desires but initiate the relationship frequently until he was satisfied. "And why don't you try to have a little fun doing it?" he concluded. "Are you suggesting that I deliberately seduce my husband? Well, of all the disgusting things I've ever heard! And from you, of all people!" And she pulled herself to her prudish height and marched angrily out of the office.

She returned several months later. She apologized for her prudish behavior and confessed that after her dignity would allow it, she cooled down, saw the logic of his proposal, and decided to follow it. It had worked. Too well, in fact. For now it was she who was the "pest" and her husband, weary and fatigued, who was losing interest. When she was able to accept the fact, during counseling, that the real problem had been her unconscious need to dominate, they were able to work out their sex problem on a mutual basis.

A year later, the counselor used this case in discussing the problem of sexual adjustment with a group of married couples. A few weeks later, he received an anonymous note from one of the wives in the group. "I just want you to know that at least one wife in that group has discovered that sexual desire is 'cumulative.' I was one of those who thought once a week was often enough. We have been having sex relations much more frequently, and I have been far more responsive than ever before. My husband is so much more cheerful and good-natured—just like the happy boy I married. And, interestingly, he is not only more affectionate and more thoughtful of me, but he has been wonderful with the children." New love-sex feeling generated by the new relationship spilled over to the children. That is as it should be. Sexual desire, when controlled by love feelings rather than physical urges, can be a truly mutual experience. Happily married couples readily accept the fact that differences of desire are inevitable, and each tries to co-operate in responding to the other's desire. Often they are surprised to find that it is a highly satisfactory experience for them also.

Broadening the *meaning* and *purpose* of intercourse lends richness, color, and variety to the experience. Especially during those periods when the couple desires to start its family and is striving for pregnancy, each intercourse might well have an almost sacred quality. But it need not be that way always.

At some times it may be a means of tension release. They may be facing an important decision and may have discussed it from many angles without reaching a decision. Intercourse, followed by a relaxed night's sleep, may make the decision seem much easier in the morning. Then there is the harassed business man who brings his problems home with him to worry about—and get ulcers from—during the night. An understanding and loving wife might well encourage him to try to verbalize the essence of the problem facing him, then entice him into activities designed to get his mind off his business and on to sexually satisfying and relaxing experiences.

Take, for example, the comment of a husband whose wife was the nervous type of woman. "When my wife gets tense and irritable with the children, the thing that helps most is to get her to have intercourse. That has taken some doing at times. When I tried to be affectionate and suggested it, she used to reply that she didn't feel like it. But if I am patient and affectionate, she finally gets aroused. At such times she usually experiences orgasm several times. The next day she is likely to be relaxed and affectionate with both me and the children."

And finally there are times when both partners are in a jolly mood, playing and having fun together. What is more natural than that this should spontaneously lead to intercourse? Or that they should cap off an evening out which has been full of fun and excitement with their own private variety?

Physical Factors to Consider

Physical factors, of course, play an important part in sexual responsiveness and enjoyment. We inherit a set of glands which determine, in large measure, along with nutrition and general health, our energy level. Some people have a great deal of energy and vitality although they may require less sleep than other members of the family. On the other hand, there may be relaxed and easygoing individuals who require a great deal of sleep and can doze off at almost any time.

This *basic energy level* plus the activity of the adrenal gland determines not only our energy level and how we react to emergency situations, but our sexual responsiveness as well.

In general, the energy level from day to day is determined by the food intake *and* the effectiveness with which that food is turned into energy. People with a high metabolic rate (hyperthyroids) turn much of their food into usable energy. Those with a low metabolic rate (hypothyroids) turn little of their food into energy, storing relatively more of it as fat in the body. A certain "emergency" supply of food is stored as blood sugar in the liver and is released for immediate use when the adrenal gland (the emergency gland) signals its need. Almost any exciting situation brings adrenal secretions which release the blood sugar and set in motion a whole pattern of physical adjustments such as increased heart beat, deeper breathing, switching of the blood supply away from the digestive tract out to the skeletal muscles and to the surface of the body.

All this is involved in sexual response. The administration of thyroid has greatly increased sexual responsiveness in many cases. Since increased consumption of thyroid, easily taken in tablet form upon a doctor's prescription, turns more food into energy and thus increases, other things being equal, the general energy level, this increased "pep" would also be reflected in the sexual urge. People who have a tendency toward overweight, even though they eat lightly, who require a good deal of sleep, who always have a difficult time achieving orgasm, and who, as one woman put it, "never want to stand when you can sit, nor sit when you can lie down," are often benefited by taking thyroid. Doctors have used metabolism tests for years to determine the individual's own thyroid output, and where it is low, have supplemented it with thyroid tablets. Now, an even more accurate test which measures the iodine content of the blood is available. No one should hesitate to discuss this matter with his or her physician.

At the other extreme, some high-geared and restless people probably have overactive thyroids. No matter how much they eat, they cannot put on weight, and so are often uncomfortably thin, and they tend to sleep only a few hours at a time. Such people can now be helped by a radio-active iodine "cocktail" which reduces the activity of the thyroid gland so that they can live more peacefully. Some of these hyperthyroid personalities have also found their sex problems reduced by such treatment.

The nervous and high-strung individual may also be that way because of psychological problems which keep him physically in a state of excitement or shock. Such persons burn up their energy and are often exhausted by the end of the day, even though they have done little. They continually burn up their emergency supply of energy stored in the liver, and so they have nothing left to go on when a real emergency or sexual activity calls for the extra "umph." The person who normally is fairly relaxed and works efficiently, but who has a good reserve is likely to respond normally to sexual stimulation.

Fatigue is likely to be associated with poor sexual response. When women are tired, they just may not have enough energy left to build up to orgasm. By bedtime many women are at their worst as sex partners. If women are at home and can take an afternoon nap, they are likely to be much more interested in sex at bedtime and much more likely to respond. Apparently, about a third of the women at home take naps while the children are taking theirs. Women should not feel lazy or guilty for doing so if it makes them happier mothers and wives.

Many couples have learned to take advantage of earlier hours of the day when energy levels are still high. Normally, women do not respond well when they first awaken. But after breakfast and a cup of coffee, they are in much better spirits. Most people have to dash to work, and so cannot avail themselves of these morning hours for sexual intimacies. But some have learned to take advantage of them on days when they can do so. In other cases, when men can take a longer lunch hour, the South American siesta after lunch has much to recommend it both as a time to relax and as a time for sexual intimacy.

New Information on Physiology as Related to Sex

Physiology is a relatively new science, but little by little much is being learned about how various organs of the body function. The sex organs have been among the most difficult and resistant to study. Animal experimentation, which has helped greatly in studying other organs, has been of little value with regard to human sex organs, for animals cannot interpret nor give intelligent co-operation.

Great progress was achieved recently with the discovery that it was possible to study sexual functions through the muscles which surround the vagina. Having found many women with both weak genital muscles and poor sexual response, Dr. Arnold H. Kegel, associate professor of gynecology at the University of Southern California, set about to find a way to strengthen the pubococcygeal muscle in as many women as possible. Then, from time to time he examined these women to note how such strengthening affected the sensitivity of the nerves that surround the vagina. Aided by the intelligent interpretations of more than three thousand women, Dr. Kegel found that sexual response is in the nature of a conditioned reflex. This means that every woman is born with potential sexual functions, or the ability to feel sexually, but the function has to be developed during her lifetime, in order that she can enjoy sexual relations fully.

Prescribing exercises to strengthen this pubococcygeal muscle (which serves as a floor to support the organs and viscera in the pelvic area, and as a sphincter muscle which aids in the control of elimination), Dr. Kegel discovered greatly increased sexual responsiveness as an interesting side effect. Apparently this muscle's range of function had eluded medical science because it had always been studied in an inactive state. Both men and women have this muscle and can discover it readily for themselves by stopping urination through muscle contraction or by drawing up the perineum as though stopping urination. Attempting to contract the vagina gives the same sensation to women because it is the same muscle contracting. Strengthening this large muscle, starting by contracting it five times, and gradually increasing it to about fifty contractions daily for a while, has, according to Dr. Kegel, often eliminated the need for surgery related to prolapse and bladder weakness, and has increased the sexual responsiveness of many women.

Dr. Kegel then developed an instrument which may be used by any woman to train and strengthen muscles that surround the vagina. The same instrument measures the strength of contractions from 0 to 100 Mm. Hg. He finds that approximately one-third of all women tested can register a change of less than 10 degrees on the dial. Another third can register between 10 and 20 degrees, and the final third with well-developed muscles can register from 20 to as much as 60 and 80 degrees. He finds that almost universally, the poorest third are the least responsive sexually, whatever sex feeling there is being associated with the clitoris rather than the vagina. The middle third is borderline. Those with the greatest muscle tone and contractual strength have the greatest sexual feeling and responsiveness, normally associated with the vagina.

Dr. Kegel's discoveries may explain why some women who have been sexually responsive before childbirth are very slow in regaining vaginal feelings afterward. In these cases, he usually finds there have been lesions in the pubococcygeal muscle which are slow to heal. The same contracting exercises have speeded recovery. Not infrequently he finds a woman with a lesion on one side of the vagina who finds intercourse pleasurable if the penis is held against the other side of the vagina, but painful or uncomfortable on the injured side. Dr. Kegel used this finding to dispose of those who would place the entire emphasis on the psychological aspects. After all, he says, the psychology is the same on both sides. She would not welcome her husband on one side and reject him on the other.

This muscle may also explain why mothers often lose interest in sex after children are born. With little knowledge of muscle physiology during or following childbirth, there is often sagging of the organs. With each additional child the condition becomes worse. After the birth of several children, intercourse becomes unpleasant. Today this situation is changing. A gynecologist recently praised the work of an obstetrician, saying, "He had delivered two children for Mrs. Jones, but when I examined her recently, there was little evidence of her having borne a child. Her muscles were firm, the organs were in normal size and place, and there was no loss of vaginal function or feeling." American women can now bear children and continue to enjoy the sexual side of marriage. Exercising and strengthening the pubococcygeal muscle, therefore, may not only help to prevent urinary or prolapse problems; it may increase the sexual responsiveness of most women and increase the pleasure for both man and wife.

Attitudes That Help—and Hinder

Sex feelings reflect, in large measure, the total feelings of two persons for each other. Therefore, anything that increases their feeling of "togetherness" normally helps to improve their sex life together. Selfishness, on the other hand, normally has a negative effect on the sex life.

If the husband, for example, acts as though the marriage license and ceremony have given him the right to have intercourse whenever *he* wishes it, he will probably soon have a resistant, or at least a frigid, woman for a wife. On the other hand, if she acts as though her sex organs were her private property, they may soon become so. If she uses sex as a sort of reward when he is a good boy and does as she wishes, or withholds intercourse when he has been "a bad boy," he may well resent being treated like a boy, instead of a man. "I think it ought to be my right to decide whether I want to have sex relations or not," one woman told her counselor. "And you are very resentful that your husband feels he has the right to have intercourse anytime he pleases, aren't you?" the counselor asked her understandingly. "I certainly am," she admitted positively. "Just how does his feeling that he has a right to have intercourse whenever he pleases differ from your feeling that you have the right to withhold intercourse anytime you wish?" he asked her. She found it extremely difficult to accept the implications of her own answer. She came to see that it was a case of mutual adjustment.

Men, as a group, are more interested in sex than women are—with exceptions, of course. The surprising thing is not that couples have problems of sexual adjustment, but that they succeed so well in adjusting them. If the woman is willing to increase her interest to more nearly match his, and he is willing to reduce his interest to more nearly equal hers, greater harmony is achieved. The wife's responsiveness and desire normally increase into the thirties and then level off until about age sixty. Males, on the other hand, normally have a relatively steady and slow reduction in sexual urge throughout their adult years. During a number of the middle years, the average man and woman have fairly equal desire.

An attitude that helps to improve sex adjustment is related to a sense of power. We discussed earlier the difference between *power over* as opposed to *power with*. This has its application in a couple's sex life too. Each sex is made more certain of its masculinity or femininity by its power to arouse a response in the other sex. From the first casual flirtations to sexual intimacy in marriage, one needs to feel capable of interesting and later arousing a response in the other. But sexual response is not something one can demand or coerce. One can exploit with *power over* but one has to *employ power with* to elicit response from one's sex partner. In exploitative sex relations, the individuals are primarily interested in their own reactions, but in love relations, one is as concerned with the other's response and pleasure as with his own. *Power with* is one key to a co-operative marriage and a mutually satisfying sex life.

Then there is the willingness to work to make the marriage succeed. Terman's study of marital happiness concluded that the most important ingredient of a successful marriage was a determination on the part of both to make it succeed. Many marital conflicts are unconscious struggles for power. Each partner wants his way—they can't both win. Rather than struggle along on the basis of compromise, the most successful marriages seem to work on the basis of unconditional giving. One yields completely to the other's wishes in one instance, and the other responds by yielding completely in other instances. Normally, people respond by loving the person who so demonstrates his or her love. Marriage is not a fifty-fifty compromise, but a willingness to go all the way when the situation demands it.

And finally, there is the determination to use sex

as a mutual *expression of love,* never as a tool or punishment. This ties in with the concept of forgiveness. One cannot change the facts of the past, but one can change their meaning. And in sensing new meaning behind the fact, one can forgive more easily. Being able to forgive and make up is a mature quality. "I'm sorry" are two of the most important words a married couple can learn. "My mother advised me never to go to sleep angry," one happily married woman told a group, "and I never have." She confided to a counselor later that for years when she and her husband had a quarrel, she would get him to make up and go to bed early. She put mutuality above the pride of being right and expressed her complete forgiveness in mutual sexual enjoyment. It might be added that this type of "making up" is not so available to men. An angry woman must be forgiven with love and affection, not with sex. But for both men and women, the tensions produced by the adrenal secretions during anger may heighten the sexual response. And such reduction of tension would seem preferable to the restless sleeplessness of stubborn people.

The Menopause

The menopause no longer means the end of a woman's sex life—it may, in fact, initiate one of the most enjoyable periods in her life. Freed of the fear of pregnancy, and warm and secure in the love of her husband, some women are able to achieve a degree of satisfaction never before quite possible. Medical science has learned much about the menopause, and much of the unpleasantness taken for granted in the past can now be minimized or eliminated by the administration of appropriate hormones, or some of the newer drugs.

Clues to the need for medical care often show up first in increased family friction—traceable to the nervousness or irritability caused by menopausal complications. Take, for example, the nineteen-year-old girl who came for help because of increasing conflict between her father and mother. When a woman who is in her forties changes from a loving and patient mother or wife into an irritable nag, a trip to a gynecologist, who specializes in female disorders, is almost the first step in treatment.

In this case, the girl read a suggested chapter on the menopause, and then discussed the situation with her father. His attitude changed immediately when he realized his wife's behavior might have a medical basis. Together they persuaded her to see a doctor, though, as she said, "There is nothing in the world wrong with me." The specialist, however, found a serious condition, and an operation followed. The operation, plus a hearing aid which made it possible for her to resume her social life and church activity, and an understanding husband and daughter, changed an irritable woman into the loving wife and mother she had been before.

Sometimes the problems are even more serious. A girl sought help from her counselor because of failing work. It soon came to light that her real problem was concern about her widowed, middle-aged mother who had become "practically impossible" and who, she had just discovered, was having an affair with a man in the neighborhood who had lost his wife the year before. The daughter was so disturbed she could not study.

As she and the counselor tackled the problem together, they decided to eliminate the menopause problem first. The daughter, in a new and more understanding frame of mind, discussed the possibility of menopause problems with her mother. "You just haven't been yourself recently. You've always been so sweet and understanding, but recently—well, you've almost made me hate you." The mother seemed to welcome the possibility of a "physical problem," and the doctor found one that yielded to treatment. Then the daughter confronted her as casually as she could with her "indiscretion" as far as the neighbor was concerned. Her mother admitted to "one last fling." She had not "had any sex life at all" since her husband had died ten years before, and she felt entitled to indulge "her last sexual desires."

The daughter helped her mother to understand that her sex life need not be over—and discussed the possibility of remarriage. The mother was surprised, for she had always felt the children would oppose remarriage. The daughter explained that she had felt that way, but that she had come to realize that it was a part of the romantic conception of a "one and only" —and that she now realized that remarriage would not be an insult to her real father, but a compliment.

The girl, on her own initiative, and unknown to her mother, called upon her mother's "boy friend." She discussed with him her mother's behavior and sought his assistance. "I love my mother and I don't want her to do something she'll regret the rest of her life," she told him. "Do you think your mother would be willing to marry me?" he surprised her by asking. She assured him she thought she would, and added that she would love to have him for a father, not having had a father for ten years. Six months later, the daughter called again on the counselor to tell him of her mother's remarriage. Naturally, not all such problems work out so well or end so happily.

Good Years in the Golden Years

A kindly neighbor with the best of intention was trying to prepare her friend for the lonely years ahead. Her last child had just married and gone to live in another city, leaving the woman and her husband alone in the old house by the river. "You'll soon find that the 'empty nest' isn't really as empty as you think it's going to be," she assured her. She was not prepared for the woman's emphatic response: "Empty nest, my eye! This is going to be a time of personal fulfillment. For the first twenty-five years I did what my parents wanted me to do. The next twenty-five years I did what my children wanted to do. This next twenty-five years, my husband and I are going to be free as air to do what we want to do." And they were. Would that all of us might grow old as actively and interestingly as they.

Free of the responsibilities for children—or for all the housekeeping they make necessary, the average woman has more choice as to how she will use her time and energy. With time to develop new interests or follow up old ones, and with the time and maturity to offer leadership in her choice of any number of community and church organizations, she may well find this one of the most satisfying periods in her life. With not only her own children, but a flock of lovable grandchildren to love, and no one but her husband to care for, she may well be a more *loving* person than she has ever had time to be before. And we are happiest when we are loving.

Her sex life may also be more "satisfying" than ever. Although her responses are slower, the deep bond of love that has grown up between her and her husband may well make their physical relations also more mellow and enriching. The sense of touch does not lose its zest, nor the afterglow its glow.

Fanning the Glowing Coals

We have all had the experience, no doubt, of sitting by a campfire or a fireplace in which the fire has died down and seems to be practically "out." Someone decides it might be nice to toast marshmallows and fans the embers to make them glow. Much to our surprise, there is far more heat left in the glowing embers than we would have imagined.

So it is with the sex life. Too many married couples assume that the fire is out and do not make the effort to fan the glowing coals. Evidence is accumulating that the more active the sex life, the longer the individuals continue to enjoy it.

General health and vitality, of course, play an important part. But is it not possible that an active sex life also contributes to general vitality? Remove the sex glands from a young stallion, and he becomes a plodding plow horse. Remove the sex gland from the rooster, and he becomes the tender-fleshed capon. Is it not true that physicians find a higher incidence of "female disorders" among unmarried women and greater incidence of prostate problems among elderly men who are not experiencing a normal sex life?

In personal conversation, a physician told of an amazing woman who had come to him in her late sixties having the problem of containing her urine. He put her on the program of exercises of the pubococcygeal muscle developed by Dr. Kegel. Not only did the exercise solve the urinary problem, but after fifteen years of sexual unresponsiveness, she began experiencing orgasm more readily than ever before. She picked up a number of activities she had dropped, and developed some new interests. She literally became a "new woman."

In Conclusion

The good life is not easily achieved. It is the result of a lifetime of dreaming, hoping, striving, accepting, adjusting, and achieving. Faith in God, in others, in life itself helps us in those moments of doubt when our faith in ourselves is shaken by the realities of existence. But without the moments of despair, our ultimate triumphs would be robbed of their deepest satisfactions.

Children make countless demands upon us. They give us, at times, a sense of utter frustration—at times they make our hearts sing with gladness. This range of feeling, and the continuous series of adjustments which each new stage of development forces upon us, is at once an agony and a blessing. Without it life would be simpler, but less satisfying.

This applies with equal force to the sexual side of life. Charged with emotion and feeling, it can be a source either of embarrassment and frustration, or of warmth and intimate sharing.

It is the hope that this book may have given parents more confidence to trust their own emotions and good sense; that it may have clarified some of the many and varied situations children and adolescents face in growing up in a bisexual world where so many of the satisfactions of life are related to the ability to work out good relations with the other sex; and that it may have, by its suggestions, released in greater measure the creative impulse in each of us that enables us throughout our life to meet new situations with courage, love, and understanding.

APPENDIX

A Few Sex-Education Books and Pamphlets
To Be Read to Young Children or by Them

Growing Up, Karl de Schweinitz (New York: Macmillan Company, rev. ed., 1953). The illustrations in the third (1953) edition of this simply written classic are enough in themselves to create good feeling for the reproduction of life. A parent can begin to share parts of this little book with children as soon as they become interested in pictures. They will enjoy coming back to it again and again as they grow up.

Into the World, Victoria Emerson and James J. Thompson (New York: Whiteside Press, 1950). An adventure story with a plot that grows in interest. Should appeal particularly to the eight- or nine-year-old girl, but also to other children. How life begins for boys and girls as well as for living things around them is skillfully interwoven into the story.

Wonderful Story of How You Were Born, The, Sidonie M. Gruenberg (New York: Hanover House, Doubleday and Company, Inc., 1952). Beautifully written and illustrated. A book that children will enjoy hearing very early and will want to reread later. The guide for parents on its jacket is very helpful.

Your Own Story, Marion L. Faegre (Minneapolis:

University of Minnesota Press, 1943, 52 pp.). A pamphlet which gives the story of reproduction for the very young child. Contains a section for parents providing sound counsel. Very helpful.

For Preadolescents

Being Born, Frances Bruce Strain (New York: Appleton-Century-Crofts, Inc., rev. ed., 1954). A book of interesting facts for boys and girls.

Growing Up and Liking It (Milltown, N. J.: Personal Products Corporation, 25 pp.). Fine, free pamphlet on menstruation.

For Older Young People

Building Sex into Your Life, Paul Popenoe (Los Angeles: American Institute of Family Relations, 5287 Sunset Boulevard, 1944, 23 pp.). Pamphlet written for young men entering the army or industry, but valuable for other young people or adults of both sexes, including parents.

Facts of Life and Love for Teen-Agers, Evelyn Millis Duvall (New York: Association Press, rev. ed., 1956). Parents who read this first themselves will be rewarded.

Finding Yourself (for ages 12 to 15) and

Learning About Love (for ages 16 to 20). See Sex Education Series on page 242.

Understanding the Other Sex, Lester Kirkendall and Ruth Osborne (Chicago: Science Research Associates, Inc., 57 Grand Ave., 1955). A Life Adjustment booklet written for the teen-ager. Better Living booklets for parents and Junior Life Adjustment booklets for upper elementary and junior high school age children, also available.

For Parents and Other Adults in
Contact with Children

Facts of Life for Children, Child Study Association of America (New York: Maco Magazine Corporation, 1954, 96 pp.). Specific answers to children's questions, preschool through adolescence.

How to Tell Your Child About Sex, James L. Hymes (New York: Public Affairs Pamphlets, 22 E. 38th St., 1949). Direct, down to earth. Inspires confidence.

New Patterns in Sex Teaching, Frances Bruce Strain (New York: Appleton-Century-Crofts, Inc., rev. ed., 1951). Even if your library does not have the revised edition of this pioneer book, the original 1934 edition would be well worth reading. It is still basically sound and refreshingly helpful.

Sex Education Series, Marion O. Lerrigo and Helen F. Southard (American Medical Association, 534 N. Dearborn St., Chicago 10, Ill., and National Education Association, 1201 Sixteenth St., N.W., Washington 6, D.C.).

Facts Aren't Enough (for adults who have any responsibility for youth) and

Parent's Privilege (for parents of preschool and

early school-age children). Excellent discussion of sex education, including facts of reproduction and sexual development. Practical suggestions as well as perspective. Well illustrated.

The three other pamphlets in this series include one for preadolescents, one for adolescents, and one for older teens and young adults.

Documentation of Books and Films
Referred To in the Text

Being Born, Frances Bruce Strain (New York: Appleton-Century-Crofts, Inc., rev. ed., 1954)

Brothers and Sisters, Edith G. Neisser (New York: Harper and Brothers, Publishers, 1951)

Building a Successful Marriage, Judson Landis (New York: Prentice-Hall, Inc., 1953)

Facts of Life and Love for Teen-Agers, Evelyn Millis Duvall (New York: Association Press, rev. ed., 1956)

Growing Up, Karl de Schweinitz (New York: Macmillan Company, rev. ed., 1953)

Handbook for Husbands and Wives, Theodore Z. Arden (New York: Association Press, 1939)—out of print but perhaps in public library

How to Be a Woman, Mary and Lawrence K. Frank (New York: Maco Magazine Corporation, 1954)

"Human Beginnings," (Association Films, Inc., 347 Madison Avenue, New York 17, N. Y.)

"Human Growth," (E. C. Brown Trust Company, 220 S.W. Adler St., Portland 4, Ore.)

Into Manhood, Roy E. Dickerson (New York: Association Press, 1954)

Marriage and Sexual Harmony, Oliver M. Butterfield (New York: Emerson Books, Inc., 1953)

New You and Heredity, The, Amram Scheinfeld (Philadelphia: J. B. Lippincott Company, 1950)

Nursery School: A Human Relationships Laboratory, The, Katherine H. Read (Philadelphia: W. B. Saunders Company, 1950)

Parent Co-operative Nursery Schools, Katharine W. Taylor (New York: Teachers College, Columbia University, 1954)

Sex Perfection and Marital Happiness, Rudolf Von Urban (New York: Dial Press, 1949)

Sexual Behavior in the Human Female, Alfred C. Kinsey and Others (Philadelphia: W. B. Saunders Company, 1953)

"Story of Menstruation, The," free to groups (International Celucotton Products Company, 910 N. Michigan Ave., Chicago, Ill.)

Teen Days, Frances Bruce Strain (New York: Appleton-Century-Crofts, Inc., 1946)

When You Marry, Duvall and Hill (New York: Association Press, rev. ed., 1953)

Wonderful Story of How You Were Born, The, Sidonie M. Gruenberg (New York: Hanover House, Doubleday and Company, 1952)